BLANDF

GW00578185

Credits

Footprint credits
Editor: Felicity Laughton
Maps: Kevin Feeney

Managing Director: Andy Riddle
Content Director: Patrick Dawson
Publisher: Alan Murphy
Publishing Managers: Felicity Laughton,
Jo Williams, Nicola Gibbs
Marketing and Partnerships Director:
Liz Harper
Marketing Executive: Liz Eyles
Trade Product Manager: Diane McEntee
Accounts Managers: Paul Bew, Tania Ross
Advertising: Renu Sibal, Elizabeth Taylor

Photography credits
Front cover: Dreamstime
Back cover: Dreamstime

Printed in Great Britain by CPI Antony Rowe,
Chippenham, Wiltshire

Every effort has been made to ensure that
the facts in this guidebook are accurate.
However, travellers should still obtain
advice from consulates, airlines, etc about
travel and visa requirements before travelling.
The authors and publishers cannot accept
responsibility for any loss, injury or
inconvenience however ca[...]

Publishing information
Footprint *Focus Red Sea & Sinai*
1st edition
© Footprint Handbooks Ltd
May 2012

ISBN: 978 1 908206 67 1
CIP DATA: A catalogue record for this book
is available from the British Library

® Footprint Handbooks and the Footprint
mark are a registered trademark of Footprint
Handbooks Ltd

Published by Footprint
6 Riverside Court
Lower Bristol Road
Bath BA2 3DZ, UK
T +44 (0)1225 469141
F +44 (0)1225 469461
www.footprintbooks.com

Distributed in the USA by Globe Pequot Press,
Guilford, Connecticut

Contents

Sinai is a mysterious land: utterly stark, wildly beautiful and intensely dramatic. Formed by a collision of continents, the austere and unforgiving mountains of the interior plummet down to meet golden beaches before melting into the coral gardens of the Red Sea. It has been said that the triangular wedge of earth, home to just 340,000 people, is but "24,000 square miles of nothing". Yet with its mystical past, dazzling seas and layers of desolate, majestic peaks, travellers fast come to find that in 'nothing' there is so much. The southern coastal region features some of the best diving in the world. Ras Mohammed National Park, at the peninsula's southern tip, is a sanctuary to every species of life that thrives in the Red Sea and a fantasy world for divers and snorkellers. Sinai's rugged interior, too, is magical. Trekkers and pilgrims journey from afar to scramble up the splendid face of Mount Sinai, gaze at the rising sun and marvel at the sacred spot where Moses received the Ten Commandments.

The western rim of the Red Sea also shelters a thriving marine life. The optimal conditions for such water delights has resulted in hasty development as epitomized by the sprawl of Hurghada, the most visited coastal resort town in Egypt. But further south lies the beguiling port of El-Quseir, where days are spent snorkelling at a nearby beach or visiting the ruined fortress, and nights are spent around campfires under a sea of stars.

The slowly widening major fault line running along the length of the Red Sea created the dramatic mountains of the Eastern Desert, a belt stretching for about 1250 km from the southern tip of the Suez Canal. These mountainous desert expanses are the final frontier before Saharan Africa and deep in their folds thrive ibex and gazelle, while nomadic tribes live a traditional lifestyle little changed in 6000 years. A safari into the interior is a quest that involves effort and time. But once there, jagged charcoal peaks and wondrous astronomical spectacles, the scattering of Roman era ruins and encounters with tribal desert life are gifts to the soul.

Planning your trip

Getting to the Red Sea and Sinai

It is possible to fly direct to Egypt from Europe, the Middle East, the USA and most adjacent African countries.

Airfares vary according to season. They peak from June to September and around other holiday times (Christmas and New Year). The cheapest times to travel are during November and January. As a rule, the earlier you buy a ticket, the cheaper it will be. It's worth checking in with a few travel agents to see if any special promotions are available and sometimes tour companies offer cheaper fares as they buy them in big numbers. Return tickets are usually a lot cheaper than buying two one-way tickets or opting for an open-ended return, unless you fly with a charter airline. Round-the-World tickets don't include Cairo on their standard itineraries and you will have to go through a company that will custom-build trips.

From Europe From London, BMI, www.flybmi.com, British Airways, www.ba.com, and EgyptAir, www.egyptair.com, offer daily flights to Cairo International airport. Flight time is about five hours and ticket prices range from £350 in the off-season to £450 during peak tourist season. You can save a bit of money if you fly indirect via a European capital (see below), usually in Eastern Europe, Germany or Greece. There are also consistent charter flights to Hurghada, Luxor and (especially) Sharm El-Sheikh, some of which leave from regional airports. Have a look at www.thomsonfly.com, www.firstchoice.co.uk, www.jet2.com and www.fly thomascook.com, as there are some great deals (as low as £50 one way if you get lucky).

There are no direct flights from Ireland and most people fly via London. Air France, www.airfrance.com, offers direct flights to Cairo via Paris. From Germany, Lufthansa, www.lufthansa.com, via Frankfurt, and TUIfly, www.TUIfly.com, are a good budget choice from Berlin, Munich and Cologne. KLM, www.klm.com, flies to Cairo from Amsterdam. Austrian Airlines, www.aua.com, Czech Airlines, www.czechairlines.com, Malev, www.malev.hu, and Olympic Airways, www.olympic-airways.com, have services too, often at competitive prices.

From North America From New York EgyptAir offers an 11-hour daily direct flight to Cairo, ticket prices range from US$1000 in the off-season up to US$1500 during peak travel times. Most European carriers offer flights from major North American cities to Cairo via their European hubs. British Airways and KLM serve the bigger cities on the west coast. From Canada, there are direct flights with EgyptAir from Montreal two or three times a week, taking about 11 hours. Some European airlines also have connecting services from Montreal and Toronto that do not necessitate overnight stays in Europe.

From Australia and New Zealand There are no direct flights from Australia or New Zealand, but many Asian and European airlines offer services to Cairo via their hub cities. Tickets can be expensive, so it may be worth opting for a Round-the-World ticket, which

Don't miss ...

could be comparable in price or even cheaper than a round-trip flight. From Australia to Egypt tickets range from about AUS$1750 during the off-season to AUS$2500 in the peak season. **Qantas**, www.qantas.com, **Austrian Airlines**, www.aua.com, and **Alitalia**, www.alitalia.com, in addition to a few Asian carriers, offer competitive prices.

Airport information   Departure tax is included in the price of airline tickets. Confirm airline flights at least 48 hours in advance. Most airports require that travellers arrive at least two hours before international departure times. Have all currency exchange receipts easily available, though it is unlikely you will be asked for them. Before passing into the departure lounge it is necessary to fill in an embarkation card. Only a limited amount of currency can be reconverted before you leave, which is a tedious process. Sometimes suitable foreign currency is not available. It is better to budget with care, have no excess cash and save all the trouble.

Baggage allowance   General airline restrictions apply with regard to luggage weight allowances before a surcharge is added; normally 30 kg for first class and 20 kg for business and economy class. If you are travelling with a charter flight or budget airline, you might have to pay for even one item of luggage to go in the hold. Carry laptops in your hand luggage, and check the airline's website to see what the restrictions are on hand luggage as this varies between different carriers.

Transport in the Red Sea and Sinai

From camel to plane to *felucca*, Egypt is equipped with numerous transport options. Congestion and chaos can be a bit anxiety-inducing on long road ventures, but with a bit of courage and flexibility, you can access most areas without too much effort. As for timetables and infrastructure, the country seems to run on magic. There are few regulations and little consistency, but somehow, people always seem to get where they want to go.

Restricted areas   Potentially risky are Egyptian border areas near Sudan, as well as off-road bits of Sinai, where landmines (usually marked by barbed wire) may exist.

Hazardous journeys

Bear in mind that Egypt currently tops the statistic charts for the highest mortality rate due to motor accidents in the world. You are taking your life in your hands on many road journeys and this is particularly true at night, when driving without headlights is the norm and buses seem to career wildly into the unknown blackness. Long-distance service taxis are the most dangerous, at any time of day, and should be taken only when there are no other options. Drivers push all limits to get there as fast as they can, so as to be able to start filling up with passengers again and complete as many return journeys as possible per day.

Air

The national airline is **EgyptAir**, www.egyptair.com, who have rebranded and became the first Middle Eastern member of Star Alliance in July 2008. In the past, foreigners paid a different (and much more expensive) price for internal flights than Egyptian residents or nationals, but now there is one ticket price for all and flying has become an affordable option for many travellers. In peak seasons, demand can be high and booking ahead is essential. You can buy E-tickets on the EgyptAir website, though it doesn't always accept the final payment. In this case, you'll have to go to an EgyptAir office or travel agent.

There are daily flights from Cairo to Sharm El-Sheikh and Hurghada and less frequently to Taba.

Road

Bicycle and motorcycle   Bicycle hire is available in any town where there are tourists, but the mechanical fitness of the machines is often dubious. Take a bike for a test ride first to check the brakes and tyres are OK. It is feasible to cycle long-distance through Egypt but the heat is punishing. In urban areas, traffic conditions make cycling a very dangerous sport. Motorcycles can also be hired, though it's less common. The problems regarding cycles apply also to motorcycles – only more so.

Bus   Buses, the main mode and cheapest means of transport, link nearly all towns in Egypt. Air-conditioned coaches ply the major routes and keep to a timetable. It's advisable to book tickets 24 hours in advance, though this is not possible in some oasis towns or from Aswan. **Upper Egypt**, **East Delta** and **West Delta** are the three main operators covering the whole country and are cheapest, usually with air conditioning and assigned seats. **Superjet** and **GoBus** also offer buses to/from most towns to Cairo, with newer and more luxurious buses that are about 30% more expensive. The downside is they play videos half the night. There are usually night buses that can save you losing a day on long journeys, and drivers always make a couple of tea-and-toilet stops at roadside coffee shops. Inner-city buses are usually dirty and crowded, and there's a jostle when the bus arrives. In the larger cities, buses often fail to come to complete stops so prepare to run and jump if you do not get on from a route's hub point. Using buses to travel from one city to another is a good way to get around but sorting out the routes of most inner-city buses makes taking the tram, subway, or a cheap taxi, a better option.

With friends like the tourist police

Those travelling around Egypt in private cars will often find themselves in the bear hug of the police authorities – mainly the tourist police. This is especially the case in Middle Egypt and Upper Egypt outside of the tourist bubbles of Luxor and Aswan. You may also come upon the free escort service when travelling between the Red Sea coast and the Nile Valley, or when exploring the Western Desert and central Sinai. Individual or small groups of foreigners find their transport under close official guard that can be uncomfortable, despite the good intentions. Officers may suggest they ride in the car with you, and if you refuse or there's not enough room, a police vehicle may follow you.

There is little that can be done to gain liberty. The Egyptian government is determined in the wake of the 1997 massacre at Luxor and bomb blasts in the Sinai that no further tourist lives will be lost to terrorist attacks. Police chiefs know that any publicized tourist deaths by Islamists in their district will mean instant transfer to an isolated village in the deep south! The best way to handle the problem is to create as profound a cordon sanitaire around your vehicle as possible; keep well out of sight line of the weapons of your watchdogs and keep as great a distance between your own car and that of your escort so as to avoid a collision. Approach the game with a sense of humour.

Car hire Vehicles drive on the right in Egypt. An international driving licence is required. Petrol (super) is E£2-3 per litre. Road signs are in Arabic, with most offering the English transliteration. Road conditions vary from new dual carriageways to rural tracks only one-vehicle wide to far flung roads that are a rough, unsurfaced *piste*. Problems include encroaching sand, roads that end with no warning and lunatic drivers. Driving at night is especially hazardous as people only put their headlights on to flash at oncoming vehicles. Likewise, driving in the major cities can be nightmarish with no margin for error and constant undertaking. If you are going to give driving a shot, make sure that you are well insured as the road accident rate is one of the highest in the world.

Car hire cost varies greatly relative to the quality of the vehicle and the location of the rental agency. The minimum is about US$40 per day, and a large deposit is generally required. Some companies place restrictions on areas that can be visited. Be aware that there are many police check points for cars in Egypt and they often request to see your papers, so have them on hand or be prepared for a hefty fine on the spot. The problems of driving your own or a hired car are twofold – other drivers and pedestrians.

The main car hire firms are **Avis**, www.avis.com and **Hertz**, www.hertz.com. See listings in each individual town transport section. To drive from Cairo to Sharm El-Sheikh takes approximately six hours.

Hitchhiking This is only really a consideration in outlying places not well-served by public transport. Rides are often available on lorries and in small open trucks but payment is often expected. Hitchhiking has a measure of risk attached to it and is not normally recommended, but in out-of-the-way places it is often the only way to travel. Solo women travellers are strongly advised not to hitchhike.

Mine peril

Thirty people die from land mine explosions in Egypt each year on average. There are estimated to be as many as 21 million land mines still in place dating from the Second World War or the several Arab-Israeli wars in more recent years. Some 16.7 million lie in the Western Desert, a damaging legacy of the long campaigns in that area in the years 1940-1943. Most of the remaining 5.7 million mines are in the Canal Zone and the adjacent battlefields of Sinai.

Most mines are anti-tank devices but, as they deteriorate with age, become unstable and are quite capable of detonating under the pressure of a human foot. Clearances and minefield marking (often merely rusty barbed wire) are going ahead slowly but meanwhile tread with care in the following areas:

1 For 30 km either side of the Alexandria–Marsa Matruh highway and all areas around the El-Alamein battlefields.
2 The open country to the west of the Red Sea such as in the deserts surrounding Safaga and Hurgada.
3 Gulf of Suez.
4 The remote areas of the Gulf of Aqaba/Sinai hinterlands.
5 North Sinai around sites such as El-Arish.
6 The Sinai passes at Mitla and Giddi.

The best advice is to stay away from locations where there are no signs of previous recent entry and always heed warning markers (posted in both Arabic and English).

Taxi and service taxi Private vehicles, often Toyota Hiaces (called microbuses or service taxis, pronounced *servees*), cover the same routes as buses and usually cost less. They and the large stationwagon-like long-distance service taxis (Peugeots), sometimes following routes not covered by buses run on the 'leave when full' principle, which can involve some waiting around. For more space or a quicker departure the unoccupied seats can be purchased. However, the drivers can be some of the most reckless in the country (particularly in the nippier Toyotas) and it is probably only worth taking them if you've missed the bus and are stuck somewhere. Inner-city taxis are smaller, rarely have a working meter, and can also be shared. In urban centres taxis are unquestionably the easiest way to get around, and extraordinarily cheap.

Sea
Ferry Ferries connect Hurghada on the Red Sea coast to Sharm El-Sheikh in the Sinai five times a week. The boats are fast catamarans so the journey takes just 90 minutes. There are daily ferries between Nuweiba and Aqaba, in Jordan.

Price codes

Where to stay

€€€€	over €150	€€€	€65-150
€€	€30-65	€	under €30

Price for a double room in high season. During the low season it's often possible to bargain the room rate down.

Restaurants

€€€	over US$20	€€	US$5-20	€	under US$5

Prices for a two-course meal for one person, excluding drinks or service charge.

Where to stay in the Red Sea and Sinai

Hotels

As tourism is one of Egypt's major industries, accommodation is widely available at the main sites and in all the major cities. With prices to suit all pockets, this varies from de luxe international hotels to just floor or roof space for your sleeping bag. There has also been a recent influx of eco-establishments popping up in Sinai and the Western Desert, a couple of which are mega-luxurious while others offer a more rustic experience. Most quality hotel chains are represented and offer top-class facilities in their rooms and business centres. There are also many cheap hotels with basic and spartan rooms ranging from the clean to the decidedly grimy. Mid-range accommodation is a bit more limited, though the occasional gem exists. There is a pronounced seasonality to demand for accommodation and in the spring, autumn and winter holiday months the main tourist areas can be very busy and the choicest hotels fully booked. Advanced reservations are recommended, especially for luxury hotels. Finding cheap accommodation is easy throughout the country, even in high season. Make sure you ask to see the room first.

Prices for the top-class hotels are on a par with prices in Europe while mid-range hotels are generally cheaper in comparison. Note that while price is a reasonable reflection of the type of hotel and service you can expect, some hotels are expensive but very ordinary while others are wonderful and quite cheap. International hotels have an uncomfortable habit of changing owner and name. Be prepared for this and if confused ask for what it was called before.

In almost every case, the advertised room price (that charged to the individual traveller) is higher than that paid by the package tourist. Bargaining is common, especially when tourism is scarce. The categories used in this book are graded as accurately as possible by cost converted to American dollars. Our hotel price range is based on a double room in high season and includes any relevant taxes and service. We try to note when a meal is included. Please be aware that prices for hotels are constantly shifting, sometimes significantly, depending on the season and the political climate. As we have quoted high season prices, expect to find costs equal to, or less than, the prices indicated. When in doubt, always ask as prices can literally be sliced in half in the hot summer months. At hotels of three-stars and higher, credit cards are almost always accepted.

Note Tax and a service charge will be added to your accommodation bill, apart from in budget hotels or unless it is clearly stated as inclusive.

Youth hostels

Information from **Egyptian Youth Hostels Association** ① *1 El-Ibrahimy St, Garden City, Cairo, T02-2796 1448, www.iyhf.org*. There are 17 hostels (in Egypt's main historic and tourist towns) that are open year round. Overnight fees range from US$1.5-9 and often include breakfast. Visitors may stay more than three consecutive nights if there's space. Although cheap meals are available, all the big hostels have a members' kitchen where guests can prepare meals for themselves (use of the kitchen is free). Rules generally include no alcohol or gambling, single-sex dormitories, and lights out between 2300-0600. Booking is recommended during peak travel times. They can be a good way to meet Egyptians, but are generally a couple of kilometres out of the centre of town and are horribly busy during student holidays.

Camping

There are only a few official campsites with good facilities and guards. Beware of veering too far off road in regions that are desolate as landmines are still widely scattered around some regions, especially near Sinai and along the Red Sea coast.

A few popular destinations, such as Dahab (Sinai), have what are misleadingly called 'camps'. These are generally very cheap and sometimes have charming grounds that offer small concrete rooms or simple bamboo huts for a few dollars per night. They often include bedding and a shared bath.

Food and drink in the Red Sea and Sinai

Forget the stories of sheep's eyes and enjoy the selection of filling, spicy and slightly unusual meals. Less adventurous, Western-style food (other than pork) can be found in many restaurants, and high-end hotels have fantastic international cuisine (but for the price you would pay at home). Basic street-stall food can be delicious, but if you are wary or they look a bit grungy, a multitude of cheap restaurants also serve local favourites often brought out *mezze*-style with a basket of bread so you can enjoy tasting a bit of everything.

Do bear in mind the suggestions in the Health section on food best avoided in uncertain conditions, see page 23.

Food

Egyptian food is basically a mixture of Mediterranean cuisines, containing elements of Lebanese, Turkish, and Greek cooking, with few authentic local dishes.

Breakfast is usually *fuul*, fava beans simmered slowly overnight, the national dish and a cheap meal at most stalls. These are served in a thick spicy sauce, sometimes with an egg, and usually in a sandwich. When it's fresh and when it's been done well, it is a mouth-watering savoury delight. Some of the best *fuul* comes from the colourful carts on wheels, which station themselves in the same places every day so hungry customers can gather round. The *fuul* is ladled out of a vast pot, hidden in the depths of the cart and heated from below, before being mashed with spices, oil, lemon, salt and pepper. Tourists rarely stop and sample a plate, but the vendors will be pleased and surprised if you do, while other customers will be highly entertained. It's probably best to avoid the chopped salad that comes with the dish, but the *ai'ish* (bread) is certainly safe enough. Equally cheap and popular is *taamiyya*, deep fried balls of ground fava beans spiced with coriander and garlic, again often served in a sandwich garnished with *tahina* (sesame seed dip) and *torshi* (brightly coloured pickled vegetables such as turnips, carrots, and limes). These constitute Egyptian fast food with the addition of *shawarma*, sliced lamb kebab sandwiches, and *fatir*, which is sold in special *fatatri* cafés, where the thin dough pancake is made to order with either sweet or savoury fillings.

Bread is the staple of the Egyptian diet, its Arabic name *ai'iish* means life. The local *ai'iish baladi*, a brown flat loaf similar to pita, tastes good fresh and should only be eaten on the day of purchase. The white flour *ai'iish shami* is less common.

Lunch is the main meal of the day, eaten anytime between 1300 and 1700. Carbohydrates, usually rice and bread, form the bulk of the meal accompanied by fresh seasonal vegetables and either meat or fish. *Mezzas*, a selection of small salads, are served at the beginning of the meal and include *tahina*, *babaghanoug* (tahina with mashed aubergines), olives, local white fetta-style cheese, *warra einab* or stuffed vine leaves, and *kobeiba*, deep fried bulgar wheat stuffed with meat and nuts. Like most Middle Eastern countries, *kebab*, lamb pieces grilled over charcoal on a skewer, and *kofta*, minced lamb, are common main dishes. Chicken and pigeon are also widely available, the latter considered a local delicacy when stuffed with rice and nuts. Fish is commonly eaten in coastal regions and often superb. Try the sea bass or red snapper but watch the bones in the latter. Lobster and shrimp are relatively cheap.

Egyptian **main dishes** include *molokhia*, finely chopped mallow leaves, prepared with garlic, spices and either rabbit or chicken, and a good deal more tasty than its glutinous texture suggests; *fatta*, layers of bread, rice, chunks of lamb or beef, yogurt, raisins and nuts, drenched in a vinegar garlic broth; *koshari*, a poor man's feast that will fill a belly for at least four hours, is composed of macaroni, rice and brown lentils covered with fried onions and a spicy tomato sauce; and *mahshi*, vegetables, typically black or white aubergines, tomatoes, green peppers, cabbage leaves or courgettes, stuffed with rice, herbs and vegetables.

Fruits, like vegetables, are seasonal although there is a wide variety available all year round. Produce is picked when it's ripe and so generally fruit and vegetables are absolutely delicious. Winter offers dates of various colours ranging from yellow to black, citrus fruits, small sweet bananas, pears, apples, and even strawberries. Summer brings plums, peaches, figs, pomegranates, guava, mangoes, grapes, melons and a brief season, for a few weeks in May, of apricots.

Traditional Egyptian **desserts** are sweet, sticky, fattening, and delicious. The best of all is *Om Ali*, or Mother of Ali, a warm pudding of bread or pastry covered with milk, coconut, raisins, and nuts. Also try the oriental pastries including *atayef*, deep fried nut-stuffed pancakes; *baklava*, honey-drenched filo pastry layered with nuts; *basbousa*, a syrupy semolina cake often filled with cream and garnished with pistachio nuts and *konafa*, shredded batter cooked with butter and stuffed with nuts. Cold rice pudding is on offer at

Fuul for all

Fuul has been an important dish for Egyptians since banqueting scenes were painted on the pharaonic tombs. It is nutritious and cheap and is the staple diet for low-income and strong-stomached locals. In Cairo a meal from one of the 25,000 (illegal) street vendors will start the day. At E£1 per sandwich it fills an empty hole and provides protein and carbohydrates.

Fuul is also considered 'in' by the Cairo smart set, who frequent luxury outlets such as Akher Saa, El-Tabei and El-Omda

to buy it with onions, pickles, lemon and fresh bread – to eat in or take away.

The *fuul* bean is grown in most agricultural areas of Egypt, as an accompaniment to a major crop – the best is said to come from Minya. Nevertheless, imports are still necessary to supply consumption demands.

Variants on *fuul* dishes include: *fuul bil zeit el harr* – with oil; *fuul bil samna* – with ghee (clarified butter); *bisara* – with oil, onion, garlic and coriander. *Fuul* is also the main ingredient in *ta'ameya* and *felafel*.

most *koshari* restaurants, and is much better than it sounds.

Vegetarianism is not a concept with which Egyptians are familiar. While vegetable dishes are plentiful, and the majority of Egyptians only rarely eat any large quantity of meat, it is difficult to avoid tiny pieces of meat or meat stock in vegetable courses. Even the wonderful lentil soup, like most Egyptian soups a meal on its own, often has the addition of a chicken stock cube. Fortunately, basic staples such as *koshari*, *fuul* and *taamiyya* are omnipresent in any town and true life-savers for vegetarians. In the smaller oases, a diet of rice, salad and potatoes or courgettes stewed in tomato sauce is tasty though repetitive.

Drink

Tea (*shai*) is the essential Egyptian drink, taken strong without milk but with spoonfuls of sugar. Tea is also prepared with mint, *shai bil na'ana*, and said to be good for the digestion. Instant **coffee**, just called 'Nescafé', is available. If you want it with milk, ask for *laban* and if you want sugar separately request *sucre burra*. The thick Turkish coffee known as *ahwa*, which is usually laced with cardamom or occasionally cinnamon, should be ordered either *saada*, with no sugar; *arriha*, with a little sugar; *mazbut*, medium; or *ziyada*, with extra sugar. Leave the thick mud of coffee grains in the bottom half of the cup. The *mazbut* is the most popular.

Other hot drinks include a cinnamon tea, *irfa*, reportedly good for colds; and the less common *sahleb*, a milk drink with powdered arrowroot, coconut, and chopped nuts.

Cold drinks include the usual soft drink options of Coca-Cola, Pepsi, 7-Up, and Fanta. Of more interest are the traditional *ersoos* (liquorice juice); *asir limon*, tangy and delicious but highly sweetened lemon juice; *karkade*, made from the dried petals of the red hibiscus, drunk both hot and cold; and *tamarhindi*, from the tamarind. Freshly squeezed juice stands are located throughout all cities, and mean you can drink seasonal pomegranate, mango, or orange juice for just E£2-3 a glass.

Bottled water is sold widely. Check that the seal is intact and that the bottle has not been refilled. Be prepared for shortage or restriction of water in more rural areas. Tap water in the urban centres is generally safe to drink, but so chlorinated it's intolerable for a lot of travellers. It's better to opt for bottled water which is cheap and easily available.

Although Egypt is a Muslim country, **alcohol** is available in bars and some restaurants. While five-star hotels are beginning to import beer in barrels, the local 'Stella' beer is the most popular sold, with the better-quality 'Stella Export', in half litre bottles. There are a few local wines, the reds and rosés are very drinkable and the whites less so. Most commonly found are Omar Khayyam, Obelisque, Cape Bay and Sherazad (who do a good rosé). The local spirits are bottled to resemble international brands, and include an ouzo called *zibib*, a rum 'Zattos', and a 'Big Ben' gin. Beware of local liqueurs that don labels and names resembling Western brands such as 'Jhony Wakker' and the like, they have been known to contain alcohol so strong that they can cause blindness if drunk to excess.

Festivals in the Red Sea and Sinai

The Islamic year (*Hejra/Hijra/Hegira*) is based on 12 lunar months that are 29 or 30 days long depending on the sighting of the new moon. The lengths of the months vary therefore from year to year and from country to country depending on its position and the time at sunset. Each year is also 10 or 11 days shorter than the Gregorian calendar. The Islamic holidays are based on this Hejarian calendar and determining their position is possible only to within a few days.

The important festivals that are also public holidays (with many variations in spelling) are *Ras El-Am*, the Islamic New Year; *Eïd Al-Fitr* (also called *Aïd Es Seghir*), the celebration at the end of Ramadan; *Eïd Al-Adha* (also called *Aïd El-Kebir*), the celebration of Abraham's willingness to sacrifice his son and coinciding with the culmination of the *Hajj* in Mecca; *Mouloud* (also called Moulid An-Nabi), the birthday of the Prophet Mohammed.

The day of rest for Muslims is Friday. Observance of Friday as a religious day is general in the public sector, though privately owned shops may open for limited hours. The main exception is tourism where all systems remain operative. Holy days and feast days are taken seriously throughout the country.

Ramadan, the ninth month of the Muslim calendar, is a month of fasting for Muslims. The faithful abstain from eating between dawn and sunset for about one month until an official end is declared to the fast and when *Eïd Al-Fitr*, a three-day celebration, begins. During the fast, especially if the weather is hot or there are political problems affecting the Arab world, people can be depressed or irritable. The pace of activity in official offices slows down markedly, most closing by 1400. You may want to stay out of the area during Ramadan and particularly the *Eïd Al-Fitr*, but for the patient and curious traveller, it can be a fascinating time. As the sun sets during the holy month and everyone rushes homeward to break fast, it offers a rare and delightful occasion to wander through barren city streets. *Iftar* (breaking the fast) in the company of local people is an interesting experience, and anyone is welcome to join a communal meal at one of the mercy tables that encroach on to the street each sunset. The country's poor are looked after by the mosques and the wealthy, who provide set meals every day for whoever is in need; this can involve feeding hundreds of people. Although you shouldn't expect true culinary delights, you might get dates, bird's tongue (a kind of pasta) soup, hearty stews and traditional sweets. For the rushed or impatient traveller, note that travel facilities immediately before and after Ramadan are often very congested since families like to be together especially for the *Eid Al-Fitr*.

Islamic festivals

These are approximate dates for 2012:

4 Feb Prophet's Birthday.
20 Jul Beginning of Ramadan.
19 Aug End of Ramadan
(Eid El-Fitr).
26 Oct Eid El-Adha.
15 Nov Islamic New Year.

Coptic celebrations

These are approximate dates for 2012:

20 Jan Epiphany.
7 Apr Annunciation.
15 Apr Easter.

Public holidays

1 Jan New Year's Day.
7 Jan Coptic Christmas.
15 Mar El Fayoum National Day.
25 Apr Liberation of Sinai.
1 May Labour Day.
18 Jun Evacuation Day –
the day the British left Egypt in 1954.
23 Jul Anniversary of 1952 Revolution.
26 Jul Alexandria National Day.
6 Oct Armed Forces' Day –
parades and military displays.
13 Oct Suez Day.
23 Dec Victory Day.

Shopping in the Red Sea and Sinai

There are department stores and malls in Cairo and Alexandria but the most interesting shopping is in the bazaars and *souks*. The process can take time and patience, but bargains abound. For a truly off-the-beaten-track shopping experience, visit one of the many fruit and vegetable *souks* scattered throughout the country. You'll find chickens milling about, people singing songs about their wares and dead cows hanging from storefront windows. Prices are clearly marked in Arabic numerals, usually indicating the cost of a kilogram. Bargaining is not appropriate in this context but learn the numerals so that nobody takes advantage of you.

What to buy

Egypt is well known for its **cotton and textiles**. Higher-end stores in luxury hotels and shopping malls sell linen and new clothes. **Jewellery**, in particular, gold, silver and some precious stones, are cheap in Egypt. Sold by weight, with a bit of money tacked on for craftsmanship, you can have pieces made to order. Particularly popular are cartouches bearing your name or the name of a friend.

Papyrus can be found, albeit of varying quality, everywhere. Ensure when you are shopping around for papyrus that it is real, not the increasingly common imitation banana leaf. Real papyrus is not chemically treated, a process which causes the picture to disintegrate after three or four years. You can tell chemically treated papyrus by its homogenous surface and pliability. Thick and unmalleable, real papyrus can't be rolled or folded. Authentic papyrus also has variants of colour as the stalks have lighter and darker patches, which you can see in the meshwork when you hold it up to the light. Rest assured that the papyrus sellers you will trip over at every major tourist site are not selling the real thing, though if you just want to pick up some cheap presents then they have their uses.

The art of bargaining

Haggling is a normal business practice in Egypt. Modern economists might feel that bargaining is a way of covering up high-price salesmanship within a commercial system that is designed to exploit the lack of legal protection for the consumer. But even so, haggling over prices is the norm and is run as an art form, with great skills involved. Bargaining can be fun to watch between a clever buyer and an experienced seller but it is less entertaining when a less-than-artful buyer such as a foreign traveller considers what he/she has paid later! There is great potential for the tourist to be heavily ripped off. Most dealers recognize the wealth and gullibility of travellers and start their offers at an exorbitant price. The dealer then appears to drop his price by a fair margin but remains at a final level well above the real local price of the goods.

To protect yourself in this situation be relaxed in your approach. Talk at length to the dealer and take as much time as you can afford to inspect the goods and feeling out the last price the seller will accept. Do not belittle or mock the dealer – take the matter very seriously but do not show commitment to any particular item you are bargaining for by being prepared to walk away empty-handed. Never feel that you are getting the better of the dealer or feel sorry for him. He will not sell without making a profit. Also it is better to try several shops if you are buying an expensive item such as a carpet or jewellery. This will give a sense of the price range. Walking away – regretfully of course – from the dealer normally brings the price down rapidly but not always. Do not change money in the same shop where you make your purchases, since this will be expensive.

You'll find **perfume** stalls as well as an abundance of fragrant and incredibly colourful stalls selling **herbs and spices** displayed in large burlap sacks. They sell everything from dried hibiscus to thyme, cumin to saffron, which is priced higher per kilo than gold, but still comparatively cheap.

Other things of interest you will find in larger *souks* and bazaars: kitsch souvenirs galore, *sheesha* pipes, musical instruments (drums in particular) copper and brass ware, wooden boxes inlaid with intricate designs and backgammon and chess sets.

Bargaining

Haggling is expected in the *souks*. Most shop owners site the start price at two to three times the amount they hope to make. Start lower than you would expect to pay, be polite and good humoured, enjoy the experience and if the final price doesn't suit, walk away. There are plenty more shops. Once you have gained confidence, try it on the taxi drivers and when negotiating a room. The bargaining exchange can be a great way to meet people and practise your Arabic.

Interestingly, a barter exchange system still exists in some rural weekly markets, where goods such as seeds, eggs or beans can be exchanged for a haircut or access to education. This is unlikely to be something you will get involved with as a traveller, however.

Local customs and laws in the Red Sea and Sinai

Though Egypt is among the more liberal and 'Westernized' of the Arab countries, it is still an Islamic country where religion is deeply embedded in daily life. While Islam is similar to Judaism and Christianity in its philosophical content and the three revealed religions are accepted together as the religions of the book (*Ahl Al-Kitab*), it is wise for travellers to recognize that Islamic practices in this traditional society are a sensitive area. Public observance of religious ritual and taboo are important, just as is the protection of privacy for women and the family. Islam of an extremist kind is on the wane in Egypt but bare-faced arrogance by visitors will engender a very negative response even among normally welcoming Egyptians who generally have no tendencies towards fundamentalist views.

Islam has a specific code of practices and taboos but most will not affect the visitor unless he or she gains entry to local families or organizations at a social level. In any case a few considerations are worthy of note by all non-Muslims when in company with Muslim friends or when visiting particularly conservative areas. (1) Dress modestly. Women in particular should see the dress code, below, for further explanation. (2) If visiting during the holy month of Ramadan where Muslims fast from sunrise to sunset, dress particularly conservatively and avoid eating, drinking and smoking in public places. (3) If offering a gift to a Muslim friend, be aware that pork and alcohol are forbidden. If you choose to offer other meat, ensure it is *hallal*, killed in accordance with Muslim ritual. (4) If dining in a traditional Bedouin setting or context, do not use your left hand for eating since it is ritually unclean. (If knives and forks are provided, then both hands can be used.) Do not accept or ask for alcohol unless your host clearly intends to imbibe. Keep your feet tucked under your body away from food.

Class discrepancies and the *khawagga* (foreigner)

Compared with other developing countries, there are particularly great discrepancies among Egyptians with regard to their experience, openness, education and worldliness. Some are extremely sophisticated, knowledgeable and well travelled while others are markedly conservative and parochial. Class is often a delineating factor, as is education and the urban/rural divide. For the traveller, maintaining awareness of social context is essential for positive and culturally sensitive interchanges with locals.

Another evident discrepancy is the cost of services for Egyptians and foreigners. If you have not yet stumbled upon the word *khawagga* (foreigner), you soon will, as it holds similar implications to the word gringo in many Latin American countries. Taxi fares, entries to many attractions, even the price of luxury accommodation all cost foreigners more. Bear in mind that the average Egyptian makes about US$1500 per head per year; the average foreign tourist lives on approximately US$32,000.

Courtesy

Politeness is always appreciated. You will notice a great deal of hand shaking, kissing, clapping on backs on arrival and departure from a group. There is no need to follow this to

Avoiding hassle

Here are some general hints to minimize the pestering that will certainly occur on some level as a woman travelling in Egypt. Try to walk with confidence and at least pretend that you know where you're going. Dress modestly – the less bare flesh the better (especially avoid revealing your shoulders, cleavage and legs). In conservative areas, don't reveal your legs at all and consider tying long hair up. Always carry a thin shawl or scarf to wrap around you in case you suddenly feel over-exposed. When swimming pretty much anywhere outside of the Red Sea resorts, wear leggings and a opaque T-shirt rather than a bathing suit. Ignore rude and suggestive comments and most importantly, avoid looking onlookers in the eye. In general, try not to react in a way that may aggravate a situation – it's best not to react at all.

When riding public transport, if possible sit next to women and avoid late-night transport if alone. If seeking advice or directions outside of hotels and other touristy places try to ask a woman or an older businessman-type. If you feel exceptionally uncomfortable, deliberate embarrassment of the man in question can be a powerful weapon – shout *haram* ('it's forbidden'). You may want to don a wedding band to dissuade potential suitors. If you're travelling with a man, you can avoid a lot of interrogations and confusion by saying that you're married. Absolutely avoid going into the desert or solitary places alone with a man you don't know.

Note that men and women in Egypt relate to one another differently from men and women in many Western countries. The Western concept of 'friendship' can be misunderstood. Opt to be conservative in the way you interact and engage with Egyptian men, as a mere smile can be misinterpreted as an expression of more than platonic interest. Most importantly, trust your instincts, be smart and keep a sense of humour. The rewards of travelling alone as a female in Egypt far outweigh any of the hassle. If you cloak yourself in baggy clothes and try to look as androgynous as possible, you'll be able to go wherever you want and be treated as a man would be, with the added bonus of everyone looking out for you just because you are a 'woman on your own'. Remember, the consequences for serious violations against foreigners in Egypt are so dire that the incidence of rape and other forms of extreme harassment and violation is significantly less than in most other countries.

the extreme but handshakes, smiles and thank yous go a long way. Shows of affection and physical contact are widely accepted among members of the same sex. Be more conservative in greeting and appreciating people of the opposite sex. Do not show the bottom of your feet or rest them on tables or chairs as this gesture is regarded as extremely rude in Egypt. Be patient and friendly but firm when bargaining for items and avoid displays of anger. However, when it comes to getting onto public transport, forget it all – the description 'like a Cairo bus' needs no explanation.

Dress code

Daily dress for most Egyptians is governed by considerations of climate and weather. Other than labourers in the open, the universal reaction is to cover up against heat or cold. For males other than the lowest of manual workers, full dress is normal. Men breaching this code will either be young and regarded as being of low social status or very rich and Westernized. When visiting mosques, *madresas* or other shrines/tombs/religious libraries, Muslim men wear full and normally magnificently washed and ironed traditional formal wear. In the office, men will be traditionally dressed or in Western suits and shirt sleeves. The higher the grade of office, the more likely the Western suit. At home people relax in a loose *gallabiyya*. Arab males will be less constrained on the beach where swimming trunks are the norm.

For women the dress code is more important and extreme. Quite apart from dress being a tell-tale sign of social status among the ladies of Cairo or Alexandria or of tribal/regional origin, decorum and religious sentiment dictates full covering of body, arms and legs. The veil is increasingly common for women, a reflection of growing Islamic revivalist views. There are still many women who do not don the veil, including those with modern attitudes towards female emancipation, professional women trained abroad and the religious minorities – Copts in particular. Jewellery is another major symbol in women's dress, especially heavy gold necklaces.

The role of dress within Islamic and social codes is clearly a crucial matter. While some latitude in dress is given to foreigners, good guests are expected to conform to the broad lines of the practice of the house. Thus, except on the beach or 'at home' in the hotel (assuming it is a tourist rather than local establishment), modesty in dress pays off. This means jeans or slacks for men rather than shorts together with a shirt or T-shirt. For women, modesty is slightly more demanding. In public wear comfortable clothes that at least cover the greater part of the legs and arms. If the opportunity arises to visit a mosque or *madresa*, then a *gallabiyya* and/or slippers are often available for hire at the door. Most women do not swim in public and if they do, they tend to dive in fully clad. If you choose to swim outside a touristy area, wear shorts and an opaque T-shirt. Offend against the dress code – and most Western tourists in this area do to a greater or lesser extent – and you risk antagonism and alienation from the local people who are increasingly conservative in their Islamic beliefs and observances.

Mosque etiquette

Do not enter mosques during a service and take photographs only after asking or when clearly permissible. Visitors to mosques and other religious buildings will be expected to remove their shoes. Men should never enter the area designated solely for women, but foreign women are tolerated in the main prayer halls of most mosques unless it is actually a time of prayer. If you are wandering somewhere you aren't supposed to be, someone will point it out to you soon enough.

Photography

Photographs of police, soldiers, docks, bridges, military areas, airports, radio stations and other public utilities are prohibited. Photography is also prohibited in tombs where much damage can be done with a flash bulb. Photography is unrestricted in all open, outdoor historic areas but some sites make an extra charge for cameras. Flashes are not permitted for delicate relics such as the icons in St Catherine's Monastery. Many museums have now banned photography completely to avoid any accidental use of flash. This includes the Egyptian Museum. Taking photographs of any person without permission is unwise, of women is taboo, and tourist attractions like water sellers, camels/camel drivers, etc, may require *baksheesh* (a tip). Even the goat herder will expect an offering for providing the goats. Always check that use of a video camera is permitted at tourist sites and be prepared to pay a heavy fee (E£100+) for permission.

Essentials A-Z

Accident and emergencies

Ambulance T123. **Fire** T125. **Police** T122 (from any city). **Tourist Police** T126.

Report any incident that involves you or your possessions. An insurance claim of any size will require the backing of a police report. If involvement with the police is more serious, for instance as a result of a driving accident, remain calm and contact the nearest consular office without delay. Some embassies advise leaving the scene of an accident immediately and heading straight to your embassy.

Electricity

The current in Egypt is 220V, 50Hz. Sockets are for 2-pin round plugs, so bring an appropriate adapter. If you have US-made appliances that use 110V it's a good idea to bring a converter. Power cuts do not happen that frequently, but in remote hotels be aware that generators are usually switched off at night and for a few hours during the day.

Embassies and consulates

For embassies and consulates of Egypt, see www.embassiesabroad.com.

Health

The local population in Egypt is exposed to a range of health risks not usually encountered in the Western world and, although the risks to travellers are fairly remote, they cannot be ignored. Obviously 5-star travel is going to carry less risk than backpacking on a minimal budget. The healthcare in the region is varied. Your embassy or consulate can advise you where the recommended clinics are.

Ideally, you should see your GP or travel clinic at least 6 weeks before your departure for general advice on travel risks, malaria and vaccinations. Make sure you have adequate travel insurance.

Vaccinations

Vaccinations are not required unless you are travelling from a country where yellow fever or cholera frequently occurs. You are advised to be up to date with **polio**, **tetanus**, **diphtheria**, **typhoid** and **hepatitis A**. **Rabies** is not generally a risk in Egypt but it has been reported in a few rural areas off the tourist trail.

Health risks

It is a very rare event indeed for travellers, but if you are unlucky (or careless) enough to be bitten by a **venomous snake**, **spider**, **scorpion** or sea creature, try to identify the creature, without putting yourself in further danger. Immobilize the limb with a bandage or a splint and take the victim to a hospital or a doctor without delay. Do not walk in snake territory in bare feet or sandals – wear proper shoes or boots. Spiders and scorpions may be found in the more basic hotels. If stung, rest and take plenty of fluids and call a doctor. The best precaution is to keep beds away from the walls and always look inside your shoes and under the toilet seat. Certain sea fish when trodden upon inject venom into bathers' feet. This can be exceptionally painful. Wear plastic shoes if such creatures are reported. The pain can be relieved by immersing the foot in hot water (as hot as you can bear) for as long as the pain persists or citric acid juices in fruits such as lemon is reported as useful.

Dengue fever is a viral disease spead by mosquitos that tend to bite during the day. The symptoms are fever and often intense joint pains, also some people develop a rash. It should all be over in 7 to 10 unpleasant days. Dengue is endemic in patches around the border area with Sudan. Unfortunately there is no vaccine against this. Employ all the anti-mosquito measures that you can.

The standard advice to prevent **diarrhoea** or intestinal upset is to be careful with water and ice for drinking. If you have any doubts then boil it or filter and treat it. Food can also transmit disease. Be wary of salads, re-heated foods or food that has been left out in the sun having been cooked earlier in the day. There is a simple adage that says 'wash it, peel it, boil it or forget it'. Also be wary of unpasteurized dairy products. The key treatment with all diarrhoeas is rehydration. Try to keep hydrated by taking the right mixture of salt and water. This is available as Oral Rehydration Salts (ORS) in ready-made sachets or can be made up by adding a teaspoon of sugar and a half teaspoon of salt to a litre of clean water. Drink at least 1 large cup of this drink for each loose stool. You can also use flat carbonated drinks as an alternative.

Pre-travel **hepatitis A** vaccine is advised. There is also a vaccine for **hepatitis B**, which is spread through blood and unprotected sexual intercourse. Unfortunately there is no vaccine for **hepatitis C**, the prevalence of which is unusually high in Egypt.

Malaria is not widespread in Egypt. Minimal risk exists in the El-Fayoum area only. Risk is highest from Jun-Oct. Check with your doctor before you go about which prophylactic (if any) you should take if travelling in this region. Use insect repellent frequently.

Protect yourself adequately against the **sun**. Wear a hat and stay out of the sun, if possible, between late morning and early afternoon. Apply a high-factor sunscreen (greater than SPF15) and also make sure it screens against UVB. A further danger in tropical climates is heat exhaustion or more seriously heatstroke. This can be avoided by good hydration.

Money

Currency ➔ *E£1 = US$0.17, €0.12 or GB£0.10.* You will see prices throughout this guide listed in either **US dollars**, **euro** or **Egyptian pounds** depending on how they're quoted in different parts of the country and for different activities. Due to recent fluctuations in the value of the US dollar, many upmarket hotels and tourist centres in Egypt (such as Hurghada and Sharm El-Sheikh) now quote their prices in euro rather than dollars. However, Egyptian pounds are used for the vast majority of everyday transactions and hotels are generally happy to accept the equivalent value in local currency.

The Egyptian pound is divided into 100 piastres (pt). Notes are in denominations of E£5, E£10, E£20, E£50, E£100, E£200, while the old 25 and 50 piastres notes and E£1 notes are being phased out. Newer E£1 coins are in circulation, and other denominations (which are almost not worth carrying) are 10, 25, and 50 piastres. It's a good idea to always have lots of pound coins to hand so you don't get short changed the odd extra pound or 2 when taking a taxi.

Regulations and money exchange

Visitors can enter and leave Egypt with a maximum of E£10,000. There are no restrictions on the import of foreign currency provided it is declared on an official customs form. Export of foreign currency may not exceed the amount imported. Generally, it's cheaper to exchange foreign currency in Egypt than in your home country. It's always wise to change enough money at home for at least the first 24 hrs of you trip, just in case. The bank counters on arrival at Cairo airport are open 24 hrs. A small amount of foreign cash, preferably US$, although sterling and euro are widely accepted, is useful for an emergency.

Banks

There is at least one of the national banks in every town plus a few foreign banks (such as HSBC and Citibank) in the big cities and Barclays have recently started operating in all major towns. Banking hours are 0830-1400 Sun-Thu (0930-1330 during Ramadan); some banks have evening hours. Changing money in banks can be a bit time-consuming, though commission is not usually charged. **ATMs** are widely available (but not in all the oases) but require a surcharge of between US$3-5, and often have a daily withdrawal limit of around E£2500-4000. They are also known to munch on the occasional card, so beware. Still, using an international credit or debit card is the easiest and quickest way to access your money and means you receive trade exchange rates which are slightly better than rates given by banks. Maestro, MasterCard, Plus/Visa and Cirrus are all widely accepted.

Credit cards

Access/MasterCard, American Express, Diners Club and Visa are accepted in all major hotels, larger restaurants and shops, and tend to offer excellent exchange rates. Outside of the tourist industry, Egypt is still a cash economy.

Traveller's cheques

Traveller's cheques are honoured in most banks and bureaux de change. US$ are the easiest to exchange particularly if they are well-known brands like Visa, Thomas Cook or American Express. There is always a transaction charge so a balance needs to be struck between using high-value cheques and paying one charge and carrying extra cash or using lower-value cheques and paying more charges. Egypt supposedly has a fixed exchange rate – wherever the transaction is carried out.

Cost of travelling

Depending on the standards of comfort and cleanliness you are prepared to accept for accommodation, food and travel, it is still possible to survive on as little as US$10-15 per person per day. However, prices for everything in Egypt are rising all the time with inflation soaring (basic foods have increased by 50%, gasoline 90%); tourists should be aware that hotel prices and transport costs continue to rise, and that the ticket prices for monuments are put up every Oct/Nov. Accommodation runs from about US$8-15 for a basic double in a liveable hotel to well over US$200 for 5-star luxury comfort. Basic street food can fill you up for less than US$1, or you can opt for a more Western-style meal, still affordable at US$6-10 a plate. Transport varies according to mode, but distances between the major cities can be covered for around US$15-20. The Cairo metro is less than US$0.25 and local buses are around the same. Renting a car is a significantly more expensive option at around US$60 per day.

There are costs often not accounted for in other parts of the world that you will inevitably encounter in Egypt. Most sit-down restaurants include a 12% tax (after the service charge, which is 10%) on the bill and it is common practice to tip an additional 10%. Another kind of tipping, known as *baksheesh*, occurs when you are offered a small service, whether or not you ask for it. If someone washes the windows of your car or looks after your shoes in a mosque, they will expect a modest offering. Carry around a stash of E£1 coins and take it in your stride, it's part of the culture.

Opening hours

Banks Sat-Thu 0830-1400.
Government offices 0900-1400 every day, closed Fri and national holidays.
Museums Daily 0900-1600 but generally close for Fri noon prayers, around 1200-1400.
Shops Normal opening hours are summer 0900-1230 and 1600-2000, winter 0900-1900, often closed on Fri or Sun. Shops in tourist areas seem to stay open much longer.

Safety

The level of petty crime in Egypt is no greater than elsewhere. It is very unlikely that you will be robbed but take sensible precautions. Put your valuables in a hotel deposit box or keep them on your person rather than leave them lying around your room. Avoid carrying excess money or wearing obviously valuable jewellery when sightseeing. External pockets on bags and clothing should never be used for carrying valuables, pickpockets do operate in some crowded tourist spots. It is wise to stick to the main thoroughfares when walking around at night.

Trading in antiquities is illegal and will lead to confiscation and/or imprisonment. Should you need to buy currency on the black market do so only when it is private and safe. Be careful as Egypt, like most countries, has tight laws against currency smuggling and illegal dealing.

Keep clear of all political activities. Particularly in light of the recent events where foreign journalists have been targeted. By all means keep an interest in local politics but do not become embroiled as a partisan. The *mokharbarat* (secret services) are singularly unforgiving and unbridled in their action against political interference.

Following the war on Iraq, there was a fairly widespread anti-American and anti-Anglo sentiment, but for the most part the disillusion is not mis-targeted. Egyptians seem to separate their disdain for foreign governments from individual travellers. Nonetheless, with such a volatile political climate, it's wise to check with your national authorities before departure for Egypt. If coming from the UK, for travel advice, check the Foreign and Commonwealth Office at www.fco.gov.uk; from the US, check the Dept of State at www.travel.state.gov.

9/11, the war on Iraq and the attacks on foreigners in the Sinai brought about a new set of challenges for the tourist industry and reinforced the government's attempts at ensuring safety for foreign visitors. Part of the system required most Western tourists travelling in private cars, hired taxis and tourist buses to travel in police-escorted convoys when journeying between towns in certain regions. This still applies in Upper Egypt, where scheduled convoys travel between Aswan and Abu Simbel. In 2010, restrictions were eased in other areas of Upper Egypt and now tourists are permitted on public transport. However, not all drivers are aware of the change in the rules and it can be a headache getting a ride in certain areas (such as Luxor to Dendara and Abydos, and along the east coast). If you want to drive, inquire with the tourist authority. See box, page 9.

Recent events According to the Foreign and Commonwealth Office website (see above), "There have been a number of incidents in Feb and Mar 2012 of kidnappings of foreign tourists and tour guides by armed tribesmen on the roads between Nuwaiba, Dahab and St Catherine's in Sinai. All those kidnapped were released unharmed within hours. There have also been incidents of robberies and roadblocks on these roads. You should exercise caution when travelling outside resorts in the Sinai and take advice from local security authorities and your tour operator".

Confidence tricksters

The most common 'threat' to tourists is found where people are on the move, at airports, railway and bus stations, offering extremely favourable currency exchange rates, selling tours or 'antiques', and spinning hard-luck stories. Confidence tricksters are, by definition, extremely convincing and persuasive. Be warned – if the offer seems too good to be true, it probably is.

Time

GMT + 2 hrs.

Tipping

Tipping, or *baksheesh*, a word you will fast learn, is a way of life – everyone except high officials expects a reward for services actually rendered or imagined. Many people connected with tourism get no or very low wages and rely on tips to survive. The advice here is to be a frequent but small tipper. The principle of 'little and often' seems to work well. Usually 12% is added to hotel and restaurant bills but an extra tip of about 10% is normal and expected. In hotels and at monuments tips will be expected for the most minimal service. Rather than make a fuss, have some small bills handy. Tips may be the person's only income.

Alms-giving is a personal duty in Muslim countries. It is unlikely that beggars will be too persistent. Have a few small bills ready and offer what you can. You will be unable to help everyone and your donation may be passed on to the syndicate organizer.

Tourist information

Depending on where you are in Egypt the provision of tourist information is variable, as is the usefulness of information provided. The offices in bigger cities tend to be quite well equipped and at least have an English speaker on duty. They're worth a visit if you are nearby. The particularly helpful tourist offices are noted in the relevant chapter sections. When the tourist offices fall short, hotels, pensions and other travellers are often even better resources to access reliable travel information.

Egyptian state tourist offices abroad

Austria, Elisabeth Strasse, 4/Steige 5/1, Opernringhof, 1010 Vienna, T43-1-587 6633, aegyptnet@netway.at.
Belgium, 179 Av Louise 1050, Brussels, T32-2647 3858, touregypt@skynet.be.
Canada, 1253 McGill College Av, Suite 250, Quebec, Montreal, T1-514-861 4420.
France, 90 Champs Elysées, Paris, T33-1-

4562 9442/3, Egypt.Ot@Wanadoo.Fr
Germany, 64A Kaiser Strasse, Frankfurt, T49-69-252319.
Italy, 19 Via Bissolati, 00187 Rome, T39-6-482 7985.
Spain, Torre de Madrid, planta 5, Oficina 3, Plaza de España, 28008 Madrid, T34-1-559 2121.
Sweden, Dorottningatan 99, Atan 65, 11136 Stockholm, T46-8-102584, egypt.Ti.Swed@alfa.telenordia.se

Switzerland, 9 rue des Alpes, Geneva, T022-732 9132.
UK, Egyptian House, 170 Piccadilly, London W1V 9DD, T020-7493 5283.
USA, 630 5th Av, Suite 1706, New York 10111, T1-212-332 2570, egyptourst@ad.com.

Egypt on the web

www.bibalex.gov.eg Detailed information and up-to-date news on the new Alexandria Library, and has a calendar of events.
www.touregypt.net A comprehensive site put together by the Ministry of Tourism. Detailed listings include online shopping from Khan El-Khalili, maps of most cities, walking routes of national parks, hotel and tour guide index and general information on life in Egypt.
www.weekly.ahram.org.eg Online version of the weekly English-language sister paper to the national daily *Al-Ahram*, extensive archive with search engine.

Visas and immigration

Passports are required by all and should be valid for at least 6 months beyond the period of your intended stay in Egypt. Visas are required by all except nationals of the following countries: Bahrain, Jordan, Kuwait, Libya, Oman, Saudi Arabia and the UAE. Cost varies between different embassies in different countries but payment must be in cash or by postal order, cheques are not accepted. It can take up to 6 weeks for some embassies to process a postal application, or they can be issued in 1 day if you turn up in person. They are valid for 3 months from date of arrival and for 6 months from date of issue and cannot be post-dated. Visas issued from embassies are either single-entry or multiple entry (which allows you to re-enter Egypt twice). Most Western tourists find it easiest to buy a renewable 30-day tourist visa (US$15 or equivalent in euro or sterling) on arrival at all international airports – but this is not possible when you are entering via an overland border crossing or a port.

For south Sinai visits, including St Catherine's Monastery, a Sinai-only visa permits a stay of up to 14 days. You can obtain a Sinai-only visa free of charge when entering through Sinai entry points of Taba, Sharm el-Sheikh airport, Nuweiba and Sharm el-Sheikh seaports. Note that Sinai-only visas are not valid for Ras Mohammed or trekking in Central Sinai.

Visa extensions can be obtained in 1 day (turn up early) at the Mogamma, Midan Tahrir, Cairo; Sharia Khaled Ibn El-Walid in Luxor; and 28 Sharia Talaat Harb in Alexandria. Some governorate capital cities, such as Ismailia and El-Tor, also have passport offices with extension facilities and these can be quite efficient places to renew (check the information under the appropriate section in the text). You will need your passport, 2 new photographs, cash to pay for renewal (cost varies depending what sort of visa, single- or multiple-entry, you require) and possibly bank receipts to prove you have exchanged or withdrawn enough hard currency to warrant your travels. Overstaying by 15 days does not matter, but after 2 weeks, be prepared for an E£153 fine and some hassle.

Entry into Israel, Palestine, Jordan, Libya and Sudan

Obtaining visas to travel in **Libya** and **Sudan** can be quite a lengthy process, and not always a sure bet, try to do this paperwork before entry to Egypt.

You can get a 1-month visa to **Jordan** on the ferry from Nuweiba to Aqaba, prices vary slightly according to nationality but it is around US$15. Crossing into **Israel**, most Western citizens can obtain a free entry visa on the border between Taba and Eilat that lasts for 3 months. However, if you intend to travel onward to Syria or Lebanon (or any Arab country apart from Jordan), you will experience problems if you have travelled through Israel first. Though Israeli border authorities will stamp a separate piece of paper, the Egyptians insist on stamping passports with an exit stamp that clearly shows which border you have crossed. For access to the current border situation, consult the respective embassy.

Weight and measures
Metric.

Contents

Footprint features

Sinai

At a glance

⊜ **Getting around** Buses around the interior and between coastal resorts; ferries to Jordan and Hurghada.

⟳ **Time required** If you want to do trekking *and* relax on a beach (especially if you're a diver), you'll need at least 2 weeks.

☁ **Weather** Sunny in winter but nights are freezing in the mountains. You'll need to take a dip in the sea to cool off in summer.

✗ **When not to go** If trekking, it's really only the cold winter nights (mid-Oct to Mar) that you may want to avoid.

Background

The Sinai has always been an most important crossroads for human expansion. Millennia ago, the Pharaohs created a path through the peninsula connecting Egypt to Jerusalem. For them, Sinai served as an easily protected barrier allowing ancient Egypt to blossom unthreatened. Later, in the third century BC, it was the stage for the Israelites' exodus out of Egypt. The Romans and Nabateans used an east–west desert route that later became the *Darb El-Hajj*, or the pilgrim's way, to Mecca. In modern times, Sinai's role as a crossroads grew even more pronounced with the completion of the Suez Canal. The strategic significance of this desert wedge and the many people that lay claim to it still yield clashes in the region, most recently in a wave of terrorist attacks by Islamist groups targeting foreign tourists between 2004 and 2006. Not surprisingly, a security crackdown ensued – but although tourist numbers decreased dramatically for a time, foreigners are now flocking back to Sharm El-Sheikh and development continues at a furious pace. It is the coastline north of Dahab, in the past lively with Israeli backpackers, that has really suffered and many of the pristine beaches now lie empty but for sagging palm-reed huts.

While most backpackers and more rugged travellers journey overland from Cairo or Israel, or by ship from Hurghada or Jordan, many now fly to Sinai direct via Sharm El-Sheikh airport. And although tourism is generating jobs and bringing in lots of foreign currency, the hasty pace of development in Sinai is of great concern to many. Since the peninsula was returned to Egypt in the early 1980s, South Sinai alone has seen the onslaught of almost 25,000 hotel rooms. The waste of perpetual construction coupled with the overload of tourists and careless divers is resulting in the rapid deterioration of Sinai's main tourist asset: the rich life of the surrounding seas. Add to this the government's North Sinai Agricultural Development Project – a multibillion dollar effort intending to relocate three million Nile Valley residents by 2017. Key to the project is the building of the Salaam canal, a huge undertaking that will transport recycled waste water and Nile water through the north of Sinai. How it will impact on the enchantment of Sinai and its Bedouin inhabitants has yet to be determined.

Warning Never allow your driver to stray off the tracks in the desert because in the national parks it is illegal and because many areas still have mines. Maps of mined areas are unreliable, mines are moved in flood waters and remain hidden. This is a general warning for all desert-border areas of Egypt and the Western Desert but is especially pertinent to Sinai.

Sinai's Protected Areas

With the Red Sea surpassing the antiquities as Egypt's prime tourist attraction, authorities are taking measures to protect the asset that is at the heart of the industry. This protection has taken the form of a network of protected areas along the coast from **Ras Mohammed National Park** (see page 36), **Nabq Managed Resource Protected Area** (see page 37), **Ras Abu Galum Managed Resource Protected Area** (see page 63) to the **Taba Managed Resource Protected Area** (see page 67), and **St Catherine's National Park** (see page 73), which covers a huge swathe of the southern mountains. With more and more tourists and developments keen to witness the beauty of this land, the presence and sustainability of the National Parks is increasingly essential to the region's survival.

West coast

The west coast of Sinai on the Gulf of Suez is far less attractive than the Gulf of Aqaba coast. It has been spoilt by the oil industry which, while being one of Egypt's sources of foreign exchange, has transformed this region into a mass of oil rigs and gas flares and made it unsuitable for another foreign exchange earner – tourism. However, the best windsurfing in Egypt draws people to Ras Sudr and a couple of short safaris into the interior are feasible from here or from Abu Zneima, removing the need to go all the way to St Catherine's for an inland adventure.

Ras Sudr

Near the northern end of the Gulf of Suez, Ras Sudr, 190 km from Cairo and 250 km from St Catherine, is both an oil company town and the site of a noxious oil refinery, and also a year-round destination for middle-class Egyptian tourists. Incessant gusts of wind throughout the day all year round make it *the* spot for windsurfing and kitesurfing. **Moon Beach** offers internationally acclaimed windsurfing opportunities and makes a good weekend break from Cairo less than three hours away.

Nearby sites include **Ain Moussa** – the springs of Moses mentioned in the Bible – and the place where the Hebrews rested after their exodus from Egypt and God provided honey dew and quails. Situated 3 km from Ras Sudr, the pool is at the foot of a small mountain where hot water springs spew out water at 26°C. There's also **Hammamat Pharaoun**, 50 km south of Ras Sudr on a 494-m mountain that rises like a natural pyramid. Some Bedouins call it *Jebel Hammam Firaun Malun*, 'the Mountain of the Baths of the Cursed Pharaoh', believing it was here the King of Egypt drowned in the Red Sea with his army when he was pursuing Moses and his people. A very hot sulphur spring spews out of the mountain at 72°C and flows to the sea. Bedouins have visited these baths for centuries to cure rheumatism. You can bathe in the steamy waters, or in the sea where they fall.

Further to the south is **Serabit El-Khadim** which, in the pharaonic period, was an area well known for the mining of the semi-precious stone turquoise and also copper. Here are the ruins of the 12th Dynasty Temple of Hathor erected for the 'Lady of Turquoise', with a small chapel to Sopdu, who was guardian of the desert ways. It's possible to arrange a tour to Serabit from Sharm El-Sheikh or Dahab, however, it is an adventure to arrange things yourself from this area. South of Ras Sudr, you will find a small port community called Abu Zenima from where it is possible to organize excursions to the lonely turquoise mines of Maghara and the temple a few kilometres further south. Bring lots of water. A reasonable amount to pay a guide is E£80 per day – not including food – and E£80 per camel, then reckon on a further E£80 to cover administration costs and fees.

El-Tur

During the third and fourth centuries El-Tur was an important Christian centre with a monastery (now in ruins) built by Justinian. But now, although it is the administrative capital of south Sinai, the seedy and dilapidated coastal town, 108 km from Sharm El-Sheikh and 170 km from Suez, has little to recommend it. It is, however, an easy and fairly efficient place to renew visas and saves a trip to Cairo. The Mugamma building is on the main road, and a visa usually takes about two hours to process if you go in the morning.

If you do end up here, have a look at the **Fortress of El-Tur**, built by Sultan Selim I in AD 1520 and the **Temple of Serabit Al-Khadim**, which stands on a small hill to the north of the town. To the east of the town are several caves such as **Cave of Hathor**, built during the reign of King Snefru, and **Cave of Souidu**, the God of War.

◉ West coast listings

For sleeping and eating price codes and other relevant information, see pages 11-15.

⬤ Where to stay

Ras Sudr *p31*

€€€€-€€€ Albatross Amira Resort & Spa, 25 km from Ras Sudr city, T017-242 4239, www.pickalbatros.com. Rather an ugly pink expanse of pink building, nevertheless the pool is huge and there are good windsurfing facilities. Rooms are clean and new, but bear in mind that (at the time of writing) alcohol is not available.

€€ Moon Beach Resort, about 40 km south of Ras Sudr, T02-3760 4050, www.moonbeachretreat.com. All bungalows have a/c and a fridge, plus there are some pricier villas. On site there is a restaurant, bar, water sports and acclaimed on-site windsurfing school with British instructors (T010-581 0088), and a kite surfing beach is a drive away. Yoga is also practised, for those of a gentler persuasion. B&B is available but as there is nowhere else to eat, it's advisable to take dinner as well. Recommended.

El Tur *p31*

€€ Delmoun, T069-377 1060. 75 rooms with a/c, private bath, breakfast included, not on the beach, best choice in the town centre. Singles E£107, doubles E£237.

⬤ Restaurants

Ras Sudr *p31*

There are a few *fuul*, *taameyya* and *koshari* restaurants in town but only the restaurants in the hotels are recommended.

⬤ Transport

Ras Sudr *p31*

Bus The daily buses between **Suez** and **Sharm El-Sheikh** stop at Rus Sudr. If you want to go to a hotel or resort further on down the road, tell the driver and he will drop you in front.

El Tur *p31*

Bus There are buses to **Cairo** at 1015, 1145, 1345, and 1615, and frequent services to **Sharm El-Sheikh**.

Sharm El-Sheikh to Dahab

The east coast of Sinai from Ras Mohammed to Taba boasts the most attractive shoreline coral reefs in the northern hemisphere. The climate, tempered by the sea, varies from pleasant in winter to hot but bearable in summer. To the east lie beaches, rugged cliffs and views to Saudi Arabia and Jordan; the west holds the barren interior.

Sharm El-Sheikh → *For listings, see pages 40-62.*

Known by locals and regulars simply as 'Sharm', this name misleadingly encompasses both the town of Sharm El-Sheikh and the resort of Na'ama Bay (6 km further north). The area has developed very rapidly in recent years becoming an international resort destination, at once glamorous and gaudy. Besides the wide sandy beaches and pristine blue sea, Sharm offers a spectacular and exceedingly popular diving area. There is over 60 km of rainbow-coloured vibrant reef teeming with hundreds of different underwater species, dramatic drop-offs and breathtaking formations unparalleled anywhere else in the diving world. The rich rugged interior is also accessible through countless tour operators eager to share the wonder of their desert with nomads of a newer and richer sort. As the region is increasingly brimming over with Western tourists, local people are accustomed to their ways; and, as a result, there is significantly less hassle on the beaches. Sharm is one of the few areas in Egypt where bikinis, beer and booty-shaking are completely the norm.

Arriving in Sharm El-Sheikh

Getting there Most travellers landing at Sharm El-Sheikh airport are already booked on a package tour. Independent travellers can take a private taxi (around E£30-100, depending how hard you haggle) 10 km to Na'ama and 17 km to Sharm. Alternatively, get a service taxi (E£5) or microbus (E£3) from the further side of the main road outside the airport. East Delta Bus buses from Cairo (470 km) to Sharm via Suez (336 km) leave from Turgoman Station, and also call at Abassiya and Al-Maza terminals. Buses terminate at the new bus station halfway between Sharm El-Sheikh and Na'ama Bay. From there, you can take a taxi (E£15-20) or take a microbus from the entrance to the bus station on to Habada (E£2, from 0630-2400). Ferries from Hurghada arrive at Sharm El-Sheikh port, from where you'll need a taxi. ▶▶ *See Transport, page 61.*

Getting around Take a microbus or taxi to travel between Sharm town and Na'ama Bay (E£2). Microbuses also run up and down the hill between Hadaba and the Old Market area in Sharm. In Na'ama, the micro effectively gets you across the bay but walking around is easy, as the area is quite compact. Getting to the bus station requires either micro or taxi. Most of the major hotels in Sharm offer shuttle buses to Na'ama Bay for free or for a nominal sum.

Information There is a barren tourist office in Hadaba that is not worth the effort of visiting, but all the major hotels can provide detailed tourist information. Useful free publications include *Sinai Weekly*, *Mix* and, in particular, *The Book* ⓘ *Viva Mall, Salem (Peace) Rd between Hadaba and Naama, T069-920 5583, T014-400 4401, www.thebook-sharm.com, open 1000-1800*, where staff provide tourist information and are very helpful. They also can issue you with a Gold Card, which is free and gives discounts in shops and restaurants in Sharm and Dahab. Useful numbers include: **Tourist Police** ① *Na'ama Bay, T069-3660311*; **Ambulance** ① *T069-920 5270-2*; and **Search and Rescue** ① *T012-313 4158*.

Sharm El-Sheikh

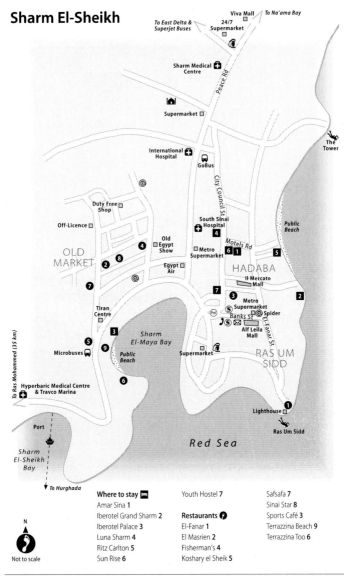

Where to stay 🛏
Amar Sina **1**
Iberotel Grand Sharm **2**
Iberotel Palace **3**
Luna Sharm **4**
Ritz Carlton **5**
Sun Rise **6**

Youth Hostel **7**

Restaurants 🍴
El-Fanar **1**
El Masrien **2**
Fisherman's **4**
Koshary el Sheik **5**

Safsafa **7**
Sinai Star **8**
Sports Café **3**
Terrazzina Beach **9**
Terrazzina Too **6**

N
Not to scale

Na'ama Bay

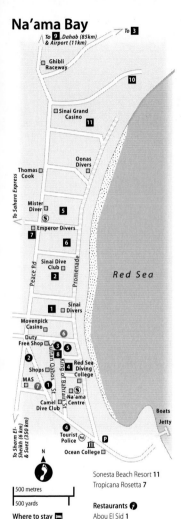

To **9** , Dahab (85km) & Airport (11km)

To **3**

Ghibli Raceway

10

Sinai Grand Casino

11

Oonas Divers

Thomas Cook

To Sahara Express

Mister Diver **5**

Emperor Divers

7

6

Peace Rd

Sinai Dive Club **2**

Promenade

Red Sea

Sinai Divers **1**

Movenpick Casino **6**

Duty Free Shop

Shops

Red Sea Diving College **4**

MAS

Na'ama Centre

Sultan Qaboos St

King of Bahrain St

Camel Dive Club

To Sharm El-Sheikh (6 km) & Suez (350 km)

Tourist Police

Ocean College

Boats Jetty

P

N

500 metres
500 yards

Where to stay
Ghazala Beach **1**
Hilton Fayrouz Village **2**
Hyatt Regency Sharm **3**
Kanabesh **4**
Marriott Beach Resort **5**
Novotel **6**
Sanafir **8**
Sharks Bay Umbi **9**
Sofitel **10**

Sonesta Beach Resort **11**
Tropicana Rosetta **7**

Restaurants 🍴
Abou El Sid **1**
Gado **2**
Hard Rock Cafe **1**
Inuka-Ya **3**
Little Buddha **4**
Viva **5**

Bars & clubs 🍸
Drinkies **6**
Tavern **7**

Sharm El-Sheikh town

The town of Sharm El-Sheikh, which existed pre-1967 as a closed military zone, was used by the Israelis. The small community, still dubbed by some 'Old' Sharm, is rapidly shedding its dilapidated image while managing to retain a relatively authentic Egyptian vibe. These days you can snack cheaply on a kebab or be refreshed at a juice stall, yet rest assured every tourist requirement will be met at a modern, attractively landscaped hotel. In the Old Market there are few scars left from the decimation caused by the bombs that killed 17 people in July 2005; the area has bounced back and souvenir stalls, super-markets and unpretentious restaurants teem day and night with a mix of Egyptians and foreigners. Cushions and rag-rugs festoon the cafés and fairy lighting is *de rigeur* along the pedestrianized strip.

Many high-quality hotels are now springing up around Hadaba, the hilltop neighbourhood between the town and resort area. While many of these cater to East European holidaymakers on package deals, there are a couple of decent mid-range places available and it's also home to an international community of dive instructors attracted by cheaper property prices and the proximity to Ras Um Sidd, a spectacular shore diving spot. Attempts to prettify Hadaba's wide waste-lands are being made as palm trees are planted along sterile highways and new buildings are settling into the landscape. While friendly little communities form around the clusters of mini-markets, coffee shops and dive centres, the Il Mercato centre – a grandiose Italianate outdoor – is a surreal reminder of the aspirations at work in Sharm.

Na'ama Bay

Purely a tourist resort, Na'ama Bay, or 'God's blessing' in Arabic, is generally considered to be more attractive than Sharm town and Egyptians are immensely proud of their 'Red Sea Riviera'. Famed for its smooth sandy beach and peaceful Corniche, huge choice of international hotels and some of the best diving opportunities in the world, Na'ama is rivalling the ancient wonders of the Nile to be the leading tourist attraction in Egypt. Relative to other locales in the Sinai, Na'ama Bay caters to tourists with money to spend. The majority of visitors are on package tours from their home countries, which often include diving opportunities in addition to airfare and accommodation, at very reasonable rates. But for a true taste of Egypt, Na'ama is lacking. In fact there is little or no indigenous Egyptian life to be found and the vast majority of hotel workers come not from Sinai but from elsewhere in Egypt. Life here has been sanitized and simplified, and the result is a plastic version of Egypt by the sea. However, saying that, it can be a pleasant change to stroll down pedestrianized streets lit by faux-Islamic lanterns, where virtually every building is low-rise and no rubbish blows in the breeze. If respite and leisure are what you seek, spectacular views across the clear blue waters of the Red Sea to the mountains of Saudi Arabia make Na'ama Bay an inviting place for relaxation, partying and playing in sea and sand. You don't have to be interested in diving but it helps, as outside of the sea and surrounding desert peaks, there is very little to see. Bedouin villages that may be of interest are more accessible from Dahab. ►► *For diving and other activities, see page 53.*

Ras Mohammed National Park

ⓘ *The national park, US$5 plus US$5 per car, is open from sunrise to sunset, as is the visitor centre, which includes a restaurant, audio-visual presentations, first aid, shops and toilets. There are colour-coded signs that lead visitors to the various attractions. Also crude toilets between Main Beach and Observatory Beach. Bring your own water bottles from Sharm El-Sheikh. Taxis to Ras Mohammed from Sharm El-Sheikh cost E£100 for 1 way but it is advisable to keep the taxi for the day – around E£150-200 – as there are no taxis at Ras Mohammed. Vehicles pass through UN checkposts. Passports are scrutinized at the Egyptian checkpoint where Israelis or any non-Egyptians who come in through Taba may experience delays. Note that Ras Mohammed is beyond the Sinai-only visa jurisdiction, so you will need a full Egyptian tourist visa to enter.*

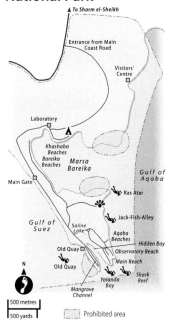

Ras Mohammed National Park

Ras Mohammed National Park, Egypt's first, was designated in 1983 and subsequently expanded in 1989. A terrestrial and marine area covering 480 sq km, just 30 minutes from the mania of Sharm, the park offers an underwater spectacle unsurpassed anywhere on the planet. Ras Mohammed is a small peninsula that juts out from Sinai's most southerly tip and is the point where the waters of the shallow (95 m) Gulf of Suez meet the deep waters (1800 m maximum) of the Gulf of Aqaba. The strong currents have resulted in a truly extraordinary ecosystem that encompasses virtually every life form thriving in the Red Sea. Besides the huge variety of brightly coloured fish that live on the coral reef, deep water species like sharks, tuna and barracuda also come to feed. Two of the reefs in the Straits of Tiran are the permanent residences of Hawksbill turtles and there are also turtle nesting beaches within the restricted areas of the park. With more than 20 acclaimed sites, the diving in Ras Mohammed is internationally renowned. (To ensure care of the area, authorities are limiting the number of dive boats coming in so try to book ahead. If you would rather dive from shore, plan to bring a diving guide and your own gear with you). The beaches around the marine gardens are also beautiful. There are some clean shallow sheltered coves perfect for snorkelling as well as more exposed stretches where wind and strong currents necessitate caution. Particularly good fossil reefs dating back 15,000 years can be found all around Ras Mohammed but are especially vivid around the mangrove channel and the visitor centre.

Ras Mohammed is remarkable too for its rare northerly mangroves that lie in a shallow channel at the tip of the peninsula, in an area with many rock pools and crevices in the fossil reef that shelter shrimp, among other stranger creatures. The famous Hidden Bay confuses visitors, because it appears and disappears with the changing tide. The Saline or Solar Lake is interesting for its range of salt-loving plants and bird watchers will also find this a delightful spot. In late summer months, thousands of white stork stop over to rest during their annual migration to East Africa. The park is also an important area for four heron species – grey, goliath, reef and greenback – as well as gulls, terns and ospreys.

Although much of the land appears to be barren and hostile it is in fact home to a variety of life, from insects to small mammals, Nubian ibex and desert foxes. The foxes are often seen near the main beaches and cubs can be spotted at sunset in late spring. They are harmless if approached but should not be fed.

Note Don't come here looking for isolation – there are over 50,000 visitors annually. Some visitors are upset by the number of boats containing inexperienced snorkellers, which scare away marine life. Come on a boat if you are a diver, so you can arrive as the sun comes up and beat the crowds – then your first dive can be enjoyed in relative solitude.

Nabq Managed Resource Protected Area

ⓘ *Entrance E£5, taxis from Sharm are E£100 for 1-way but it is advisable to keep the taxi for a half-day at around E£200, most hotels organize day trips.*

Nabq Managed Resource Protected Area, 35 km north of Sharm El-Sheikh, is also an outstanding area (designated in 1992) of dense mangroves – not only the largest mangrove forest in Sinai but the most northerly in the world. The area covers over 600 sq km around Wadi Kid, at the edge of which are rare sand dune habitats and a swathe of *arak* bushes, still sold in bundles in the village markets and used for brushing teeth. The presence of the mangroves has allowed multiple ecosystems to develop, sheltering more than 130 plant species and a diverse selection of wildlife. Storks, herons, ospreys and raptors are quite common (the area is recommended for birdwatchers); mammals like foxes, ibex and gazelles are more rare. The hyrax, a small rodent-like mammal which is actually the closest living relative to the elephant, can be found here in Wadi Khereiza. The area's sandy bottom make it a great place for swimming and the diving is good although there is risk of sediment and the reefs lie at some distance meaning that diving is better from a boat and not from the shore.

A small Bedouin settlement, **Ghargana**, lies on the coast where the tribesmen continue to fish in a traditional manner. Here are some teashops and cafés where tourists are welcome. Another Bedouin village, **Kherieza**, is inland from the main coastal valley Wadi Kid. The parks make a sincere effort to involve the Bedouin in their work and to protect their traditional lifestyle, currently under much pressure from the rapid development in the area. Near the settlement is a more modern establishment, a shrimp farm that supplies much of the produce for the hotels and restaurants in Sharm El-Sheikh.

Though popular with safari groups, Nabq is significantly less crowded than Ras Mohammed, but the beaches are decidedly inferior and it is generally much windier.

Dahab → *For listings, see pages 40-62.*

Dahab, meaning 'gold' in Arabic, still manages to shimmer despite the march of progress. Once known for its laxness with regard to marijuana, unfathomably cheap accommodation and food, and a super-chilled backpacker vibe, people used to come here to get stoned, go diving, and kick back – for weeks at a time. Though the place is still Dahab, things have changed. The Sinai tourist authority, with the hope of bringing in more money and the tourists who have it, have initiated a 'Sharm-ifying' of the area and required many establishments to trade off their beach-front cushions and Bedouin-style seating areas for 'proper' tables and chairs. Fancier hotels have sprouted up, offering a wider range of accommodation for a wider range of humanity, wooden stalls have turned into marble-fronted shops, and everywhere offers a massage or a jacuzzi. The changes haven't impacted on the entire bay, though, and many proprietors have been creative and managed to retain the former flavour. Newcomers and old-timers will still find beach cafés, bazaars and mosques amid crumbling concrete camps and palm trees. Thankfully, despite the influx of construction and tourism, the magic of the sea, sun and stars remains unsoiled. Dahab is still a gem of a place where time dissolves into tea and smoke and the ever-changing colours of the surrounding peaks.

Arriving in Dahab

Getting there Dahab is 98 km north of Sharm El-Sheikh, 82 km from Sharm El-Sheikh airport, 133 km from Taba and 570 km from Cairo. Very few daily buses run north from Sharm El-Sheikh and south from Taba and Nuweiba, service (shared) taxis leave when full, or private taxis can be hired from the main towns in Sinai. East Delta runs daily buses to Dahab from Cairo through Suez and Sharm. Buses arrive in the bus station in Dahab City in the south. To get to Assalah, a pickup taxi (which will be waiting) will transport you for around E£5-10 depending on how many people are with you.

Getting around Dahab can be divided into two distinct areas: the Bedouin village, **Assalah**, and the administrative 'city' of Dahab about 3 km south. Assalah is further divided into three parts: the actual village where locals live and the adjacent tourist areas of **Masbat** and **Mashraba** where travellers hang out. There are also a few self-contained resorts on the

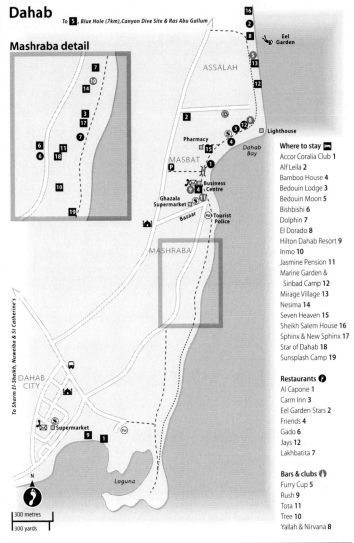

Dahab

To **5**, Blue Hole (7km), Canyon Dive Site & Ras Abu Gallum

Mashraba detail

ASSALAH

Eel Garden

MASBAT

Pharmacy

Dahab Bay

Lighthouse

Business Centre

Ghazala Supermarket

Bazaar

Tourist Police

MASHRABA

To Sharm El-Sheikh, Nuweiba & St Catherine's

DAHAB CITY

Supermarket

Laguna

N

300 metres
300 yards

Where to stay 🛏

Accor Coralia Club **1**
Alf Leila **2**
Bamboo House **4**
Bedouin Lodge **3**
Bedouin Moon **5**
Bishbishi **6**
Dolphin **7**
El Dorado **8**
Hilton Dahab Resort **9**
Inmo **10**
Jasmine Pension **11**
Marine Garden & Sinbad Camp **12**
Mirage Village **13**
Nesima **14**
Seven Heaven **15**
Sheikh Salem House **16**
Sphinx & New Sphinx **17**
Star of Dahab **18**
Sunsplash Camp **19**

Restaurants 🍴

Al Capone **1**
Carm Inn **3**
Eel Garden Stars **2**
Friends **4**
Gado **6**
Jays **12**
Lakhbatita **7**

Bars & clubs 🍸

Furry Cup **5**
Rush **9**
Tota **11**
Tree **10**
Yallah & Nirvana **8**

water just south of Dahab City in an area known as the **Laguna**. Walking is really the best way to get around, but there is no shortage of pickups and taxis. A taxi costs E£10 from one section of town to the other, pickups are a bit cheaper, depending on the number of passengers. You can always bargain or wait for another ride to come along.
▸ *See Transport, page 61.*

Places in Dahab

The changes to Dahab have brought some benefits. The town is still very cheap and significantly cleaner. A boardwalk has replaced the dust path connecting the jumbled mass of beach restaurants, camps and safari centres. There is abundant access to the necessities of modern life – internet, banking, post, telephones. The tourist restaurants are, for the most part, very clean and many of the bathrooms actually have toilet paper. With more bona fide safari companies emerging, Dahab serves as a notable set-off point for serious desert trekking to explore Sinai's mystical oases and exquisite rock formations, but it's primarily a diving and chill-out zone. Local Bedouin offer camel trips into their nearby villages; visitors will doubtless be invited for a cup of spiced Bedouin tea in their homes. The protected area of **Ras Abu Gallum** (see page 63) lies to the north and **Nabq** (see page 37) to the south. Both are easily accessible and offer enchanting tastes of Sinai terrestrial and aquatic wilderness. **Assalah**, the Bedouin village and its nearby surroundings remain a good place to experience the richness and beauty of Bedouin culture and to take time out (or in) for as long as life allows. ▸ *For What to do, see page 58.*

Note Smoking pot in the open is essentially a thing of the past (though you never really know what is burning on the coals of a *sheesha* pipe) and tourist police maintain a subtle but persistent presence. Since growing marijuana is not illegal for Bedouins, but selling it is, it's still around. Bear in mind that the penalties for drug use and possession are severe.

◉ Sharm El-Sheikh to Dahab listings

For sleeping and eating price codes and other relevant information, see pages 11-15.

▭ Where to stay

Sharm El-Sheikh *p33, map p34*

For the budget-conscious backpacker, Sharm and Na'ama have little to offer in the way of affordable accommodation except for the EYHA. The majority of sleeping options are at least 4-star and the few cheaper places that do exist are overpriced for what they offer. Rooms are significantly less expensive if they are booked as part of a package or tour.

The town of Sharm El-Sheikh encompasses several neighbourhoods that offer accommodation ranging from the average to the elegant. Most hotels are located in either **Ras Um Sidd**, close to the famous dive site and lighthouse, or the residential clifftop area known as **Hadaba** (meaning 'hilltop'), which contains many middle-of-the-road hotels that may be cheaper but are, for the most part, nothing special. Though most of these places have shuttles to private beaches and are well equipped with many amenities including their own pools, there are much better deals to be had so shop around a bit. When the season is not saturated with tourists or there is war brewing nearby, you may find the more luxurious hotels offer competitive rates. Have a look online. **Sharm El-Maya**, the waterfront area encompassing the downtown part of Sharm El-Sheikh, has a couple of hotels enjoying the advantages of beachfront accommodation and proximity to the traditional shopping area of Old Sharm.

In the spring and autumn, when the tourist season peaks, it is advisable to make advance bookings for the higher-end hotels and budget accommodation, as both extremes are the first to fill up.

€€€€ Ritz Carlton, Ras Um Sidd, T069-366 1919, www.ritzcarlton.com/sharmelsheikh. The 1st Ritz on the continent is still the most de luxe hotel in Sharm and has every amenity imaginable and then some. All 88 sea-view rooms have been refurbished, also garden-view rooms, beach access, award-winning restaurants – each with a different theme, **La Luna Italian** is a must – athletic facilities, diving centre, luxurious spa and candle-lit evenings gazing out to sea.

€€€ Iberotel Grand Sharm, 1 km from Ras Um Sidd, T069-366 3800, www.iberotel-eg.com. On a coral beach equipped with floating jetty to facilitate entry into water. Pools, restaurants, disco and athletic facilities. Good snorkelling, dive centre, and beautiful views of the sea and Tiran Island.

€€€ Iberotel Palace, Sharm El-Maya bay, T069-366 1111, www.iberotel-eg.com. Sparkling 2-tier pool among lush foliage and bougainvillea, adjacent sandy beach and a quick stroll to the Old Market.

€€€ Luna Sharm, City Council St, Hadaba, T069-366 5650, www.lunasharm.com. This place bustles with Brits and the poolside music is somewhat loud, but it's known for its friendliness, capable staff and community atmosphere. Price includes breakfast, and half- and full-board are available.

€€ Amar Sina, Hadaba, Motels Rd, T069-360 0777, www.minasegypt.com. Moorish architecture with dusky domes and kitsch courtyard spaces make this a good choice in Hadaba. Each room is different, there's a decent pool and jacuzzi. **Colona Dive Club** is reputable and particularly popular with Scandinavians.

€€ Sun Rise Hotel, Hadaba, Motels Rd T/F069-366 1725. A good mid-range option, so book ahead as it gets busy. Clean, fresh rooms and a decent-sized pool surrounded by flowers. Restaurants, shuttle bus to beach and **Sinai Rose** diving centre is adjacent. Half-board available.

€ Youth Hostel, Hadaba, near the police station, T069-366 0317, sharm.bookings@ egyptyha.com. The cheapest place to stay in Sharm by a long shot, beds in 3-bed dorms are E£55 per person, doubles E£60, for single person occupancy E£115, includes breakfast. Rooms are better upstairs with balcony, the view from the back is good, however many rooms have an unpleasant odour and plumbing can be hit and miss. Open 24 hrs. Often full during Egyptian holidays, it's recommended to book via email.

Na'ama Bay *p36, map p35*

The number of hotels in Na'ama Bay continues to grow. The longer established ones extend back from the boardwalk to the main road and some offer marginally cheaper rooms across the Peace highway. Almost every hotel has its own tourist office offering water sports equipment, diving information and desert safaris. Stretching north from Na'ama is a string of resort enclaves, all the way to the protected area of Nabq. Again, the best deals to be had are through tour companies before you arrive. Accommodation for the budget conscious in Na'ama Bay is close to nil, the nearest is in Shark's Bay or at a couple of mid-range places that chiefly accommodate divers. Breakfast is included at all the places listed below.

€€€€ Camel Hotel, King of Bahrain St, T069-360 0700, www.cameldive.com. Comfortable and convenient, book ahead as space is limited to 38 rooms. Camel keeps expanding and improving, and as well as the **Roof** bar (the place for late-night drinking among the diving fraternity) there's now the excellent **Tandoori** restaurant and a good Italian. Rooms are large, very clean and nicely (if boringly) decorated, with terraces/balconies, TV and fridge. Disabled rooms available. Free Wi-Fi.

€€€€ Ghazala Beach, centrally located on the bay plus a sister hotel across the highway, www.redseahotels.com. This old-timer in Na'ama was the tragic scene of one of the 2005 bombs; after renovations, no physical scars remain save for strong security. Rooms are either apartment style in the main building or in cabanas in the garden (preferable). An assortment of restaurants indoors and out represent different cuisines, bars offer happy hours (**Beir Wagen** has Swiss cuisine), huge central pool plus separate and peaceful 'relax pool' for adults only, instant access to beach and all facilities.

€€€€ Hilton Fayrouz, centrally located, T069-600136, www.hilton.co.uk /fayrouz. One of the oldest and most picturesque hotels in Na'ama Bay, it offers double bungalow rooms in lush gardens, with the largest private beach, a playground for children, several bars with happy hours, excellent food, cyber café and Wi-Fi, 1st-class water sports (and dive centre), yacht, glass-bottom boat, pool, tennis, minigolf, beach volleyball, horse riding, massage, aerobics, disco, games room.

€€€€ Hyatt Regency Sharm, T069-360 1234, www.sharmelsheikh.regency.hyatt.com. Beautiful hotel with exquisite gardens overlooking the sea. Beach is coral laden, not ideal for swimming, but pools are fabulous. Disabled rooms, plush public lounges and a lot of marble. Excellent Thai restaurant, some say it's the best place to eat in the bay.

€€€€ Marriott Beach Resort, T069-360 0190, www.marriott.com. Spacious, modern hotel has recently expanded with additional rooms across the Peace highway, large free-form pool, connected by wooden bridges and surrounded by sun terrace and gardens, spectacular waterfall in the central courtyard. In standard Marriott fashion, it offers all amenities including watersports equipment rental, dive centre and a health club. Particularly popular with wealthy Egyptians.

€€€€ Novotel, T069-360 0172, www.novotel.com. Extremely large yet surprisingly appealing hotel, rooms with terrace or balcony among landscaped gardens, choice of good restaurants, tennis, pool that often plays loud music, attractive stretch of private beach .

€€€€ Sofitel, T069-360 0081, www.sofitel.com. A sophisticated hotel with large pool, diving centre and the Near Coral Gardens just off shore. Health club, sauna, jacuzzi, Turkish bath and massage, table tennis, archery (pay locally) and mountain bikes for hire. Shows and entertainment provided by in-house professional team. The Indian restaurant is superb and the inspiring view of the Arabian mountains makes it an excellent place for an evening cocktail.

€€€€ Sonesta Beach Resort & Casino, at the northern edge of Na'ama Bay, T069-360 0725, www.sonesta.com/SharmResort. Overlooking the bay, it's a good place to enjoy an evening drink or stay in one of the cool collection of white domes in extensive gardens. Attractive and spacious, the hotel has 7 pools (some heated and some not), dive centre, shops and boutique. The 520 split-level rooms are decorated in Bedouin style with either balcony or patio. Selection of cuisine, including **La Gondola** Italian and **Tandoori** Indian restaurants, several cafés and bars, children's club (5-12 years – runs daily 1000-1600), tennis, squash, spa, 24-hr babysitting service.

€€€€-€€€ Tropicana Rosetta Hotel, across Peace Rd, T069-360 1888, www.tropicanahotels.com. Best known for the excellent **Emperor's Divers**, it offers comfortable accommodation with satellite, a/c, good Egyptian restaurant, **Shades/Night Magic** disco, mall, laundry and cyber café.

€€€ Eden Rock, T069-360 2250-4, www.edenrockhotel.net. Perched on the cliff overlooking Na'ama Bay, this is a smart boutique hotel with a great pool area and a private beach. Amazing views, good bar area, something a bit different for Sharm. Walking up and down the cliff when it's hot is the only annoyance.

€€€ Kahramana, T069-360 1071-5, www.balbaagroup.com. Fresh, white, bright, good value and hence very popular, this hotel has sizeable rooms all with balcony or terrace (nicest by the pool if you don't mind noise), plus 10 suites. There are 3 bars, including swish 'Fly' lounge bar on the roof as well as a nice Italian restaurant, kids' club and full services including dive centre. A 3-min walk to the beach.

€€€ Kanabesh Hotel, T069-360 0184, www.kanabeshvillage.com. A more modest option with rather old-fashioned a/c rooms in pleasant grounds, lots of loungers on the roof, right next the private beach with a great choice of restaurants that aren't overpriced. Quieter than most places though it's in the thick of things.

€€€ Oonas Hotel, T069-360 0581, www.oonasdiveclub.com. Very decent, if small, rooms all with balconies (plus 4 suites), in a great position at the northern end of the bay. There's a large private beach, loungers on the hillside and a garden. Predominantly home to divers, but super-friendly to all-comers, the restaurant is reasonably priced and the **Razala** rooftop bar is just right for a quiet sunset and *sheesha* moment. Show your *Footprint Handbook* for a 10% discount on hotel, diving and courses.

€€ Naama Inn, T069-360 0801/5, www.naamainn.com. Decent-sized rooms with new showers, not all have terraces, small pool, attractively landscaped, private beach a short walk away. About the cheapest you can find in Na'ama, popular with Egyptians, no alcohol served, free Wi-Fi. Dive school attached.

€€-€ Sharks Bay Umbi Diving Village, 6 km north of Na'ama Bay, 10 mins (E£20) from airport by taxi, T069-360 0942,

www.sharksbay.com. 3 levels of accommodation, ranging from basic bamboo huts with clean communal showers (hot water) to the domed Bedouin-style chalets on the hillside. There's an excellent restaurant in a tent by the beach where the speciality is, unsurprisingly, seafood. Coral garden for snorkelling is directly off the beach and the very popular dive centre (run by Bedouin and international staff) offers affordable courses and equipment. Camel, jeep and desert safaris are available if you get bored with the view of Tiran Island.

Ras Mohammed National Park
p36, map p36
It is possible to camp (**€**) in designated sites inside the national park, but it is camping of the rugged sort, with no showers. It costs about E£100 to be dropped off from Sharm by taxi and there is an entrance fee of E£5 per person with an additional E£5 fee for cars. Bring everything you will need including water, as it may not be available. Also note that the park is beyond the jurisdiction of the Sinai-only visa, so plan to come here only if you have obtained a tourist visa that covers all of Egypt, and bring your passport.

Dahab *p38, map p39*
Note A good website, where you can book cheap hotel deals online, is www.dahab.net.

Nowadays Dahab offers something for everyone. There are a few high-end resorts near Dahab City and the lagoon, these are quite self-contained and intentionally separate from the Bedouin village. Their prices fluctuate depending on the season. There's a range of comfortable middle-price options in Assalah; for US$50, expect a/c, a pool, and all the usual 4-star amenities.

Assalah is still a budget traveller's dream, with a few camps offering bungalows and concrete box rooms for less than US$6, or a dorm bed for US$3. For about US$10 per night, you can find a comfortable double room with fan and private bath. Along the beachfront there are dozens of 'campgrounds' varying from slightly run down to exceedingly pleasant. Camp quality varies though all, or parts of all, have electricity, sit-down toilets, hot water, fans and usually a/c. For the sake of security, opt for padlocked rooms or bring your own lock. It's tough to find a bamboo hut these days as most camps now have concrete rooms, expect to pay E£20-40 per person per night. If you want the private bath and maybe fan or a/c, the price varies from E£40-100 per night depending on extras. Many camps offer a discounted breakfast, some only have hot water in winter. Think about what's important to you, keep in mind mosquitoes and peeping toms and look around. Don't drink the tap water – it's brackish and hard. Prices in Dahab for everything are always negotiable and better deals can be made in the low season. If you plan to stay a month or more, say so in advance and many camps will give you a good deal.

Dahab town

€€€€-€€€ Hilton Dahab Resort, near the laguna, T069-364 0310, www.hilton.com/worldwideresorts. A fully self-contained resort of whitewashed rooms with domes and seductive hammocks on their terraces. Large diving centre (see www.sinaidivers.com), excellent windsurfing and aquasports centre, tennis, central pool (swimming is not permitted in the decorative lower levels!). Travel agent organizes excursions into desert, 3 good restaurants and **Coconut Bar** on the rooftop. It's the snazziest hotel in Dahab though quite isolated from the pulse of Assalah. Off-season, there are bargains to be had when rooms can go down to US$120 per couple, see www.hotels4you.com.

€€€ Accor Coralia Club, on the lagoon, T069-364 0301, www.accorhotels.com. Attractive bungalow rooms spaced out among lush gardens, good for kite and windsurfers (there are both German and British schools operating from the beach). Superior rooms are newly done out (kitsch Moroccan style) with huge sea-facing balconies, the cheaper garden-view rooms get booked up fast. 2 restaurants, bar, pool (no shallow end), ATM, tennis courts, massage, bicycle hire, volley ball, horse riding, safari and desert trips, diving centre, non-residents can enjoy the pool (but not other facilities) for E£50.

Mashraba

Most camps and hotels in this area have views across the Gulf of Aqaba. Mashraba tends to be quieter and more popular with families and couples. Unlike Masbat, most establishments here have been able to retain the old-style Bedouin seating areas and flavour. All the places below include breakfast in the price, unless otherwise stated.

€€€ Christina, T069-364 0390, www.christinahotels.com. A mid-range mid-sized hotel, with a larger than average pool and well-established garden making the grounds feel quite lush, There's a rooftop restaurant on the sea. A variety of rooms including cheaper ones across the road, away from the sea.

€€€ Nesima Hotel, T069-364 0320, www.nesima-resort.com. One of the nicest places to stay in Assalah, and certainly in Mashraba. Rooms are classy yet cosy, with domed ceilings (even in the bathrooms), some with wheelchair access, some with breathtaking views across the Gulf. There's an elegant restaurant, poolside bar and a popular night-time bar with happy hours and live football. The dive centre is well-established and there's beach and reef access.

€€ Star of Dahab, T069-364 0130. Has reef access and a beach with traditional seating where one can truly gaze at the stars of Dahab. Rooms are all pine and fresh paint with big balconies looking out to the sea. A good breakfast is included.

€€-€ Inmo Hotel, T069-364 0370-1, www.inmodivers.de. One of the 1st hotels in Dahab, this is a quality place owned by a German-Egyptian couple. 4 categories of room, all unique, range from chic and luxurious with private terrace to clean 'backpacker'- basic with shared bath. Some rooms are in elevated wooden chalets. Has a sweet little pool area, children's play area, all-round good atmosphere and fills up fast (particularly rooms with balconies on the seafront) so book ahead. Primarily known as a divers' hotel, they also organize desert safaris with local Bedouin guides.

€€-€ Sphinx and **New Sphinx**, T069-364 0458, www.sphinxdahab.com/www.sphinx-hotels-dive.com. 2 hotels next door to each other with the same owner, they are fairly similar but the original **Sphinx** has just been newly remodelled so try there first. Both are very acceptable, with pools and dive centre. The beachside restaurant, **Funny Mummy** is surrounded by palms and thick with fairy lights, with a roof-top area, which makes an agreeable venue for dining, plus there's a bar.

€ Bedouin Lodge, T069-364 1125, www.bedouin-lodge-dahab.com. Popular and well-established with freshly decorated rooms (with fan E£80, with a/c E£100 per double) and an unpretentious atmosphere; many guests here are divers. Good views of the sea from the pricier rooms, cosy restaurant is especially inviting at night when lit by candles, and serves some Bedouin dishes, plus beer and sheesha. Bedouin-run and family-friendly. camel, snorkelling and jeep trips arranged.

€ Bishbishi, T069-364 0727, www.bishbishi.com. Although located across the road from the beach, this camp has become a mecca for backpackers as the owner, 'King' Jimmy, succeeds in reviving some of the essence of old Dahab. Rooms are arranged around a garden attractively planted with date palms, there's a cushioned slouching area and plenty of seating, book-swap, bikes

(E£40 per day), safaris and trips pretty much anywhere arranged, snorkelling equipment (E£10) and a good menu that's cheaper than most. The range of 40 rooms, with/out attached showers, fans or a/c, are very clean and characterful, with comfortable beds, doubles range from E£50-130. A particularly safe camp for women travelling solo, and there's a real mix of nationalities.

€ Dolphin, T069-364 0258, www.dolphin camp.net. One of very few places that still has some huts made of wicker (shared bathrooms) as well as concrete options (some with private bath), very clean and well maintained though landscaping is minimal and a few plants would be welcome. Conveniently and centrally located while maintaining a peaceful air, there's a good restaurant out front and breakfast is included in the price.

€ El Salem, www.elsalemdahab.com. Arranged around the original Bedouin stone house, El Salem has some bare basic rooms for E£50 a double (just beds) and quaintly decorated rooms at the front with a yoga theme (E£85), shared bathrooms. For an en suite the price goes up, but all is negotiable. Yoga 4 times per week and a hippy vibe.

€ Ghazala, T069-364 2414, www.ghazala dahab.com. Domed ceiling rooms, blue and white bedspreads, good value at E£100 per double with fan or a/c E£140. Arranged in 2 facing rows across a central aisle, giving a cosy homely feel but noisy if other guests are hanging out.

€ Jasmine Pension, T069-364 0852, www.jasminepension.com. Small but well-appointed rooms, some with sea view, are good value in this newish hotel. Staff are friendly without being overwhelming, and they're willing to strike a bargain. The relaxing restaurant is a good spot to start the day, serving decent coffee, excellent juices, lassies and generous breakfasts.

€ **Jowhara**, Mashraba St, T069-364 0079, www.jewelofdahab.com. Friendly Bedouin place that's been going 25 years, with recently updated large rooms that are especially clean and fresh. Great value, particularly for standard fan rooms (single E£50, double E£70, triple E£100). Surprisingly quiet though on the main road (away from beach), around a garden with palm trees, nice new café. Desert trips easily arranged. Very pleasant and helpful management.

€ **Sunsplash Camp**, T069-364 0932, www.sunsplash-divers.com. This long-standing camp, chiefly catering to divers from Germany and returning guests, has moved with the times and the wicker huts are spotless, most now have bathrooms, a/c and heat, and there's a hotch-potch of wooden rooms at the front. Once peacefully located on the edge of Mashraba, the camp is now crowded by new-builds but you can still, within a few strides, snorkel the house reef. Anita, the owner, speaks English, German and Arabic and organizes trips into the desert away from the crowds. Look for the quirky bright blue wooden huts by the boardwalk, which cost E£80.

Masbat

Masbat is where most of the action lies. Bars, restaurants blaring Arabic pop, tourist bazaars, hawkers selling everything and nothing and dazzling fairy lighting all loom large. However, most accommodation stretches quite a way back from the promenade and is possible to search out tranquillity.

€€€ **Alf Leila**, El Fanar St, T069-364 0595, www.alfleilahotel.com. Dahab goes boutique in this gorgeous Arabic-style B&B. The 8 rooms are individually designed and themed, using rich colours and Islamic motifs. Sadly it's next to the main road rather than the beach (10 mins' walk) but some might feel that's a good thing. Fabulous German bakery on the ground floor.

€€ **Bamboo House**, T069-364 0263, www.bamboohouse-dahab.com. More attractive inside than out, this hotel in the midst of things has only 7 rooms meaning it's a good idea to call ahead. All rooms have satellite TV, fridge and a/c. Breakfast included.

€€-€ **Alaska**, T069-364 1004, www.dahab escape.com, This well-run operation has simple rooms that are spotlessly clean, as are the en suites. On 2 levels, they are more expensive with a/c and balcony, doubles range from E£90-180. Friendly staff, free Wi-Fi, safaris and trips easily arranged. Recommended.

€ **Fighting Kangaroo**, T069-364 2747, sbulti@gmail.com. Homely, low-rise little 'camp' with plain but clean rooms, very good value (hence often full). Shrubs, creepers and a quiet atmosphere, without hoards of divers. Communal fridge and kitchen for guests' use, safaris/trips are competitively priced.

€ **Seven Heaven**, T069-364 0080, www.sevenheavenhotel.com. Deceptively large camp in the centre of things, very popular with Japanese divers, they have a huge variety of rooms for all backpacker budgets. Top-end with private bath, a/c or heat and a balcony are actually unattractive, but a great deal are the E£40 rooftop rooms with views (shared bath) while a bed in the a/c dorm is E£20. All rooms include fan and screens on windows, but the shared bathrooms could be cleaner. Internet E£5 per hr, Wi-Fi access is not free, laundry, 10% off rooms for divers, and loads of trips on offer to virtually anywhere.

Assalah

The shoreline north of the lighthouse is dotted with an array of accommodation ranging from cheap camps to more comfortable middle-of-the-road accommodation, all with sea access and loungers on the 'beach'. The vibe turns a bit hippy and New Age as you wander north.

Inland lies the non-touristy village where Bedouin, other Egyptians and long-time foreign implants live.

€€€-€€ Blue Beach Club, T069-364 0411, www.bluebeachclub.com. There's some tasteful styling in this comfortable hotel, with Arabic lamps and blue glass casting a cool light in the rooms. Pay more for with sea views, though the extension across the road (mountain views) actually has nicer rooms with brand new fixtures and fittings. All have a terrace or balcony. Yoga, diving, horseriding and, of course, massage are on offer.

€€€-€€ Dive Urge, T069-364 0957, www.dive-urge.com. An intimate place with 10 well-maintained rooms arranged around a flowery garden. Some have sea views, others have domed ceilings, quirky shapes, pine furniture and bright Mediterranean colours. The beach area has chairs and tables, nearby access to the Eel Garden and on-site dive centre. Run by a British-Egyptian couple plus helpful staff.

€€ Mirage Village, T069-364 0341, www.mirage.com.eg. Comfortable rooms have some nice touches and decor is muted though rather brown/beige, with fridge, a/c, newly tiled bathrooms and floors. Fine views and beach access, away from the bright lights, a more mature and peaceful air pervades, breakfast included.

€ Marine Garden Bedouin Camp, T069-364 0211, www.marinegardencamp. com, and **Sinbad**, T069-364 1005, next door both retain the feel of a proper old-school camp. Rooms are simple and spartan, but with clean linen, around well-raked courtyards decorated with the odd mural. Plenty of seating/cushions and hanging out space, use of the kitchen, attracts long-stayers. Rooms at **Marine Garden** are E£60/80 without/with bath, while **Sinbad's** cheapest are tiny rooms with shared bath (hot water) at E£35/45 single/double, larger E£50/65, plus some rooms with bath at E£85.

Assalah to the Blue Hole
€€ Bedouin Moon, T069-364 0695. Beautiful Bedouin-owned and run hotel situated solemnly amid mountains and sandy beach. Rooms have private bath and domed ceilings, a/c, more expensive for a sea view. Highly acclaimed dive centre, **Reef 2000**, attached. Excellent restaurant. A few kilometres north of Masbat, good place to stay if you're here for the diving and peace.

🍴 Restaurants

Sharm El-Sheikh p33, map p34
In addition to the standard buffet-style hotel offerings, there are several good restaurants in town that are frequented by both local and foreign tourists. These days, it's hard to hunt out genuine, cheap local eateries serving *fuul* and *ta'ameyya* sandwiches; easier to spot are *kushari* and *kofta* stalls.

€€€ El-Fanar, at Ras Um Sidd lighthouse, T069-366 2218, www.elfanar.net. Under Italian management, serves excellent, albeit pricey, food with a variety of wines. The atmosphere is majestic, open-aired, with a stunning view of the sea and mountains of Ras Mohammed. There is live music most evenings. A fantastic place for sunset.

€€ El Masrien, Old Market area, T069-366 2904 (home deliveries), www.el-masrien.com. Always packed with Egyptian families feasting as well as a sprinkling of tourists, this institution has plenty for vegetarians alongside its famed skewered meats. Noisy indoor seating as well as plenty of outdoor table space. The most popular place to eat in the Old Market. Soon to open a branch in Nabq.

€€ Fisherman's, Old Market area. Primarily another seafood joint, but in addition serves up some Western, Russian and Egyptian dishes. Enjoy a beer (they ask for E£20 but will go down to E£15) amidst fairy lighting.

€€ Safsafa, market area. Delicious seafood, only 10 tables, no alcohol, meals starting at around E£35. Has a counterpart in Na'ama

Bay – but this is the original and people in the know say it's better, as well as cheaper.

€€ Sinai Star, on the pedestrianized street, T069-366 0323. Open 1100-0100. Offers excellent grilled fish in generous portions. Prices have increased over the years, but it's still better value than most others and has outdoor seating and a cave-effect interior. They don't serve beer but you can bring your own from the off-licence next door.

€€ Terrazzina Beach, next to Iberotel Palace, T069-366 5046. Enjoy fresh and excellent seafood with your toes in the sand, then chill in the Dahab-style area with a *sheesha*. It costs E£50 if you wish to lounge on their patch of beach from 0900-1900.

€€ Terrazzina Too, Harbour Rd, Sharm El-Maya, 300 m further along the bay from **Terrazzina Beach**, T010-1477 577, www.terrazzina.com. Table seating over the water or Bedouin-style cushions, this specialist fish restaurant has daily offers (fish or seafood meals plus a beer for US$9-15), fish is imported daily from Alexandria, and they also do Italian food. Entry to the beach is E£100 Sun-Thu (includes towel, mattresses, umbrellas). On Fri, when a beach party goes from 1300-2100, it's E£150, on Sat when the party is 2300-0400 it's E£120 (includes a beer or soft drink). A good mix of nationalities, watersports also on offer.

€€-€ Sports Café, Horus Mall, Habada, T014-400 4552. Open 1000-0300. Handy café, near the Il Mercato Mall, with free Wi-Fi. Western and Egyptian food is tasty and the menu quite varied, and they do excellent *sheesha tufah*. Screens show sporting events, and there's outdoor seating. No alcohol.

€ Koshary el Sheik, near the microbus stand opposite the Tiran Centre, is cheap and tasty for koshary and other Egyptian staples.

Na'ama Bay *p36, map p35*
€€€ Abou El Sid, in front of the Naama Centre, T069-360 3910. Not as magical an environment as the original venue in Cairo, but the fabulous Egyptian/Oriental cuisine matches up.

€€€ Hard Rock Café, next door to **Abou El Sid**, T069-360 2664, www.hardrock.com/sharm. Regular Hard Rock offerings and atmosphere, good nachos and Mexican/Southern cooking (mains E£35-90), children's menu, opens at 1200, the bar gets kicking after midnight and the disco keeps going until very late.

€€€ Little Buddha, Tropitel Na'ama Bay Hotel, T069-360 1030, www.little buddha-sharm.com. Sushi and Asian fusion cuisine in sophisticated surroundings, worth a splash. Hard to see what you're eating in the dim lighting, and best to go early otherwise the music and crowds will certainly distract.

€€€ Rangoli, at the Sofitel, T069-360 0081. Excellent Indian in a splendid setting with a stunning view out to sea. But arrive early (open 1900) as after 2100 the animation team gets loud and ruins any chance of romance.

€€€ Sala Thai, Hyatt Regency, T069-360 1234. Offers authentic and delicious cuisine, either on terraces overlooking the sea or in the wood-carved interior. Pretty special.

€€ Al Dente, Novotel Hotel. The pasta dishes are great and the menu ambitious, in a relaxed and attractive waterfront setting.

€€ Cilantro, T16313, this reliable café has branches at the **Hilton Fayrouz** and on the Sanafir Promenade. It feels overpriced but it is good for light meals and good coffee.

€€ Peking, Sanafir Hotel. An Asian restaurant that has undergone many incarnations since its original inception to become something of an Egyptian institution. Serves decent, though not necessarily authentic, Chinese food. Part of the Peking chain that has several branches in Cairo.

€€ Tam Tam, Ghazala Hotel. Has long been known for excellent Egyptian and Lebanese food and has a large selection of salads – both local and conventional – in a pleasant beachfront location. There are regular folkloric shows in the evenings.

€€ **Viva Beach**, on the promenade, www.viva.sharmnet.com. Open 0900-0200. Beachside restaurant where E£30 gets you a lounger, towel and loud music for the day (but don't expect sophistication). Meals are generous, adjacent **50 Bar** has karaoke and sports while **Lavita** roof bar has DJs (house and r'n'b) and gets messy later on.

Except for fast food, there are no cheap eats in Na'ama. The most-rock bottom is the imaginatively named € **Koshary**, on Sultan Qabos St, where a rather average *kushary* comes in at E£5-8.

Dahab *p38, map p39*

The traditional places to eat and chill out have always been the beachside cafés, on bright coloured cushions or close-to-the-ground chairs. Menus are quite similar from café to café though each place offers a different atmosphere, and many have blazing fires on a windy night. If you're looking for a buffet meal or high-end indoor eating experience, check out the restaurants at the **Hilton** or next-door **Swiss Inn**. Most hotels open their buffet dinners to non-residents.

Mashraba

€€€-€€ **Lakhbatita**, on the promenade in Mashraba, T069-364 1306. Offering a wide array of authentic Italian dishes and world cuisines. Romantic atmosphere indoors, which is interestingly decorated with doors and dusty oddments from the Delta. Newly decorated outdoor seating area a metre from the sea, but not as busy as it once was.

€€€-€€ **The Kitchen**, T019-595 9764, www.thekitchendahab.com. Indian, Chinese, Thai and sushi cuisine in a glossy setting on 3 levels (a/c or open air), nicely lit and atmospheric, food is OK value with mains starting from E£35 and going up to E£75 for some of the seafood. Can bring your own alcohol.

€€ **Aqua Marine Creperie**, on the promenade. Open from 0900. Savoury (steak!) or sweet (E£15-30) crêpes with good combos of ingredients, Italian coffee, good juices (E£15).

€€ **Dolphin Café**, next to **Dolphin Camp** in Mashraba. In addition to solid breakfast fare, the dinner menu includes Indian and vegetarian dishes for under US$5, Bedouin-style seating, good samosas and curries – a refreshing respite from the normal Dahab fare (the naan is a little less authentic).

€€ **Jasmine Pension**, T069-364 0852, www.jasminepension.com. A laid-back restaurant on the water's edge with a menu that contains few surprises, but the Dahab standards are better than average and the prices reasonable. Definitely a good choice, particularly popular at breakfast time.

€€ **Nesima Hotel**, T069-364 0320. The restaurant serves alcohol and delicious food and is surprisingly inexpensive. The atmosphere can feel intimate, if you choose the right seat.

€€ **Dahab Restaurant**, T069-364 0118. Good for simple Egyptian fare, such as roast chicken meals, *koftas*, and veg/beans, all served with rice, *tahina* and salad.

Masbat

Bedouin seating in this area has given way to low tables and chairs in most restaurants. Beyond the bridge is a string of gaudily lit but attractive seafront restaurants, which all have similar prices and similar menus. Some might employ more pushy touts than others, but generally they are lively and friendly places where you're likely to end up at some point. Smaller, more eclectic eateries tend to be on the other side of the promenade away from the sea.

€€€-€€ **Blue Beach**, 1st floor above at Seven Heaven. This Thai place might look un-prepossessing, but the dishes are wonderfully authentic as the owner comes from Thailand; always busy with local expats in the know. Chicken forms the core of the menu and makes a refreshing change from fish. Vegetarians are also well catered for, however, with soya as well as vegetable options available. Recommended.

€€€-€€ Carm Inn, T069-364 1300. This chi-chi place lives up to its name, Bedouin Arabic for 'small oasis and place of bounty'. Delectable dishes from all over the globe, including India and Indonesia, with inventive vegetarian options, are served in an softly lit grotto among palm trees. Highly recommended.

€€€-€€ Friends, T069-364 0232. Has a very pleasant atmosphere and keeps a more Egyptian style to its decor. Beach-side setting, good music, excellent service and extensive salad bar. The food is consistently good and the fresh juice isn't watered down or sugared up. Free Wi-Fi.

€€ Jays, at the northern end of Masbat, T069-364 1228. Great food with an extensive menu, always a veggie option, fresh menu every night, tasty desserts. Atmosphere is pleasant with Bedouin-style seating and palm trees.

€€ Nirvana, Masbat. Lots of folk enjoying their beach area with recliners during the day, and and night it's a fine place to eat decent Indian dishes. Veg/meat thali is E£100/120, main dishes (E£40-65) come with raita, rice, bread and salad.

€€€-€ Leila's German Bakery, at Alf Leila B&B, El Fanar St, Masbat, T069-364 0594. This is a really quality place to indulge any cravings for Western delights such as black-forest gateau, apple strudel and sinful pastries.

Assalah

€€€-€€ El Dorado, T069-364 1027, www.eldoradodahab.com. Wed-Mon. Italian-managed restaurant and café serves up authentic meals, particularly good pasta isn't cheap (E£65-75), though yummy pizzas are good value (E£45-50) and there are some meat delicacies (E£70-100). The beach area

has attractively laid-out loungers beneath woven parasols, with great access to the Eel Garden.

€€€-€€ Eel Garden Stars, friendly restaurant in quiet pristine setting, with excellent access to snorkelling. Lots of crêpes, expensive breakfasts but generous portions, excellent food, try the fried aubergines. BBQ night on Fri at 1900.

Bars and clubs

Na'ama Bay *p36, map p35*
Nightlife in Sharm largely centres around Na'ama Bay, with the exception of a couple of places in Nabq and the **Soho Square** complex near the airport, where you can visit the **Ice Bar** (made entirely of ice) for a shot of frozen vodka.

Bus Stop, King of Bahrain St. Open until the wee hours with lots of noise, screened football,pool tournaments, karaoke and r'n'b nights. Pick up a flyer to see what's on.

Camel Bar/The Roof, Camel Hotel, T069-360 0700. Open 1700-0200, earlier if there's major sporting event on TV. Buzzing most evenings. A funky and happening spot with typical bar fare, good music and reasonably priced drinks. Very popular with divers and beer enthusiasts, young and old. The Roof bar is a bit more chilled.

Fly, Kahramana Hotel roof, T014-666 9266, Bar-lounge with cocktails. It's a good pre-clubbing venue from 1900-0200.

Hard Rock Café, in front of the Naama Centre, T069-360 2664, www.hardrock. com/sharm. With a family-friendly atmosphere in the early evening, the bar starts raging later alongside dance music in typical Hard Rock fashion.

Little Buddha, Na'ama Bay Hotel, T069-360 1030. Definitely the most stylish place around, with a cooler crowd sprawled on the comfy seats or grooving through the subtle lighting. The party gets started around 2330 and entry is free.

Pacha, www.pachasharm.com. A vast venue what was the Sanafir hotel, with Ministry of Sound nights at weekends, House Nation on Thu, Ladies Night is Mon and Tue night is Cherry Drops Pool Party. Whatever night, the tunes are pumping.

Pataya, T014-533 3118, Nabq. Wed is foam party night, starting 2300, on the beach.

Rawsha, Oonas Dive Club. Open 1700-0100. Rooftop bar that's relaxing and chilled with great sunset potential. Not so busy because it's a bit of a walk along the bay. Sheesha available.

Tavern Bar, www.thetavernbar.com. One for the regulars, this perennially popular place shows football on a large screen and serves up a lot of steaks.

For a more traditional evening, there are plentiful cafés and *ahwas* offering *sheesha*, Arabic music, tea, coffee and often beer lining the 2 main pedestrianized streets. Several off-licences mean you can have a cheaper beer on your balcony.

Dahab *p38, map p39*

Nightlife mainly revolves around the restaurants and hotel bars along the promenade that are open until people leave, plus a couple of places where people get dancing later on.

Furry Cup, Blue Beach Club, Assalah, T069-364 0411. Open 1200-late. The closest thing to a real pub, equipped with TV showing football, attracts the British/expat community in the main. There's a happy hour from 1800-2000 and also a beach bar.

Mojito, off the promenade in Mashraba, has a Mexican restaurant on the beach, a sports bar and Dahab's only 'club' at the rear. Party night 4 times a week (in high season), starts in the bar at 2200 and then moves into the club from 2400-0500, entrance free though drinks are pricey.

Nesima Hotel bar, Mashraba. Popular, particularly with divers; happy hour from 1900-2100. There is a DJ on some evenings.

Rush, Masbat. Retains a slightly more refined air at a cool location near the bridge, playing a mix of decent tunes. Nice garden environment.

Yallah Bar, at the northern end of Masbat, always attracts a crowd of drinkers of an evening. There's a beach seating/loungers (very popular during the day) or indoor bar with upstairs area that is a good spots to watch the world go by. Happy hour 1800-2200.

Entertainment

Sharm El-Sheikh to Dahab *p33, map p34, p35 and p39*

Casinos

Na'ama Bay has several late-night casinos based mainly in the hotels. Oldest among them is the **Maritim Jolie Ville's Casino Royale**, open 24 hrs, while the immense **Sinai Grand Casino** on Peace Road presents further temptation. Bring your passport if you intend to gamble.

Shows

Oriental floorshows and bellydancers are largely confined to the major hotels but another (free) option is the Old Egypt show, 2100-2400 nightly, by the market in Sharm El-Maya. The waterfalls and theatrically lit cliff become quite attractive in the half-light and the atmosphere is jovial.

Shopping

Sharm El-Sheikh *p33, map p34*

Souvenirs are significantly cheaper in Old Sharm than in Na'ama Bay. The best-stocked supermarkets in town are: **24/7**, just off Peace Rd near Viva Mall, Hay El-Nour – you'll need a taxi or minibus; and **Metro** supermarket opposite EgyptAir at the bottom of the hill near the old market. There is a duty-free shop in the Old Market, where a tax-free allowance is valid for the 2 days following your arrival.

The Tiran Centre in Sharm El-Maya bay offers upscale shops and chain restaurants. In Hadaba, the Il Mercato mall is saturated with all things Western and all to the tune of piped soft-rock music. The nearby Alf Leila centre attempts a more rustic feel and sells all the standard souvenirs among some open-air hang-outs for a beer or *sheesha*.

Na'ama Bay *p36, map p35*
Most shops in Na'ama Bay are linked to the hotels and are well stocked with provisions for beach lounging or diving and snorkelling accessories. Tourist shops abound, selling T-shirts, perfume bottles, *sheesha* pipes, Bedouin jewellery and the rest. There are duty-free shops, where a tax-free allowance is valid for the 2 days following your arrival.

There's also a plethora of shopping strips that offer more conventional stores. The Na'ama Centre, on the northern side of Na'ama Bay, is overflowing with fashion and jewellery shops as well as chain restaurants.

You can hire an underwater camera at most diving centres. There are several digital stores (which also develop photos) scattered throughout Na'ama Bay.

Bookshops
Bookshops in Maritim Jolie Ville, Ghazala and Fayrouz Hilton hotels.

Dahab *p38, map p39*
Several supermarkets, open 0730- 2400, stock all the basics including bottled water and toilet paper. Fresh fruit and vegetables are harder to come by. Ghazala supermarket, near the police station is well equipped with most of the essentials.

Necklaces, tie-dyes, skirts and bags etc, the hallmark souvenirs of Dahab, are available in the small bazaars on the main bay and by the taxi drop-off. Don't shop when the Sharm El-Sheikh tourists are in town – everything doubles in price. Barter hard. You'll find spice stalls, carpet sellers,

lamp shops and music shops blaring the latest Arabic hits and offering a wide range of Western and traditional music.

⚠ What to do

Na'ama Bay *p36, map p35*

Bowling
MAS, just up the hill opposite Hard Rock Café, T069-360 2220.

City tours
Very dense day trips are on offer to Cairo for around US$150-275 (depending on whether travelling via bus or plane) and Luxor (0600-2130) for about US$275. If you're trying to cram Egypt into your beach experience, you may want to explore this option, but a hectic and exhausting day does only allow the merest glimpse of Egypt proper. Day trips are organized by Sun N Fun (see page 58), as well as the Sonesta Beach Resort (see page 42), among others.

Desert safaris
It is possible to book day trips and tours to see parts of Sinai's breathtaking desert interior. Most hotels in Na'ama Bay offer a sort of desert safari, but for the most part they're intended for tourists who want to look through the window of an a/c bus and the experience can be shared with quite a crowd. A tour to St Catherine's Monastery (10 hrs), which may include a trek to the summit of Mount Sinai and a visit to a Bedouin village costs from US$40-100 depending on content and number of people. For US$50, a jeep will transport you to Wadi Ain Kid, a lush canyon filled with fruit trees and funky rock formations just 40 km north of Na'ama. Or for about US$60, you can visit the enchanting Coloured Canyon and take the hour-long hike to its depths. If you're interested in a more extensive, authentic and rugged desert experience, a better plan is to set off with a real Bedouin guide from Dahab or Nuweiba.

Responsible diving

There has been a great deal of unnecessary damage caused to the coral reefs around the coast. Divers taking trophies, anchors being dropped onto the living corals, rubbish being thrown into the water. The regulatory bodies set up to prevent this damage to the environment have had little effect – it is up to those who delight in this area to preserve it for the future.

Code of responsibility for reef divers:

- Check you have the correct weights. As the Red Sea is a semi-enclosed basin it has a greater salt content than the open ocean. The extra salinity requires heavy weights, thus buoyancy checks are essential.
- Avoid all contact with coral. These living creatures can be damaged by the slightest touch. Many reef fish are inedible or poisonous – but the reef needs them to survive.
- Remove nothing from the reef. Shells and pieces of coral are an integral part of the reef. In Egypt this is taken so seriously that boat captains can lose their licence if either shells or pieces or coral are brought on board.
- Always move with care. Careless finning stirs the sand and can smother and kill the softer corals.
- Do not feed the fish. Introducing an unnatural imbalance to the food chain can be fatal and is thus prohibited.
- Be mindful in caves. Air bubbles trapped in caves can kill the marine creatures who extract their oxygen from the water.
- Do not purchase souvenirs of marine origin. Aid conservation, do not encourage trade in dead marine objects, which is illegal in Egypt.

Diving

Water sports in general, and diving in particular, are the main attractions in south Sinai. The reefs off the Gulf of Aqaba coast are some of the best in the world with incomparable coral reefs and colourful marine life. The waters are warm year round, currents are relatively benign and visibility is consistently good. Most divers from Europe book a package before they leave, including diving courses and safaris in combination with accommodation and airfare. This is usually the most economical way to go. If you are an independent traveller, there is no shortage of dive centres available to accommodate you. Most of Sinai's main dive centres are based in Na'ama Bay but organize day-long offshore dive trips to all of the region's major reefs. Many also book week-long live-aboard safaris that traverse the wonders of the Red Sea. Dive centres generally organize all transport to and from Sharm. All offer courses ranging from the beginner's Open Water to instructor level. A standard Open Water course costs €300-390 and takes 4-5 days. Often the certification requires an extra fee of €30, and the manual is about €30. PADI is the most common certificate granted and a world-known diving accreditation. Do your research before you commit to a dive school, as some are safer and more reputable than others. Be aware that some dive schools try to cram the open-water course into as little as 2 or 3 days. Though it may be cheaper, we do not recommend it. Most large hotels have their own dive centres, the following is a list of some good choices.

Camel Dive Club, centrally located in Na'ama Bay, T069-360 0700,

Wrecked ships

Satellite images indicate over 180 wrecks on the bed of the Red Sea. By far the most wrecks are to be found around the dangerous Straits of Gubal at the mouth of the Gulf of Suez. Access is easiest from Hurghada or Sharm El-Sheikh.

Thistlegorm was a 126-m-long, 5000-tonne English cargo ship that was damaged on 6 October 1941 by a long-range German bomber and sank without firing a defensive shot or delivering her goods to the awaiting British troops fighting in the North Africa campaign. Nine of the crew lost their lives. She lies on the massive Sha'ab Ali reef, on the northern edge of the Straits of Gubal, under 30 m of water just as she went down, complete with an incredible cargo of armaments. There are jeeps, trucks, motorbikes, tanks, train cars, a locomotive and an 'explosive' collection of ammunition, along with uniforms and regulation boots. She was 'discovered' by Jacques Cousteau in 1956 but visits by casual divers to this war grave only began in the late 1990s.

Dunraven, an 8-m sail-equipped steam ship has been lying on the reef of Sha'ab Mahmood just south of Beacon rock since 1876. She is now covered with soft corals and sponges and each year looks more attractive. She lies bottom up with the bow 15 m and the stern 28 m below the surface, her journey from Bombay to Newcastle-upon-Tyne incomplete. This English merchant ship carrying a cargo of spices and exotic timber is now home to lion fish and other colourful inhabitants.

Carnatic, once a 90-m luxurious Greek steamship, is a sad tale. With a passenger list numbering 230 and a cargo of gold reported to be then worth £40,000, she hit the reef at Shab Abu Nuas on 13 September 1869. The conditions were calm, the ship remained upright and life for the passengers remained as normal until the vessel snapped in two without warning – 27 people were drowned. £32,000 worth of gold was rescued, but where is the rest? Perhaps it is still there waiting for a lucky diver. The abundance of sponges and corals and the favourable light conditions make this popular for underwater photography.

Giannis D was another Greek vessel, 99 m long and full of cargo. She ran aground on the reef at Shab Abu Nuas on 19 April 1983 and later broke in two and sank. The shallowest remains are just 8 m under the surface allowing easy access to the bridge and the engine room in the stern. *Giannis D*, covered with soft corals, is considered one of the best wreck dives.

Aida II was sunk in 1957 to the north-west of Big Brother Island. The stern section of this supply ship, all that now remains, is encrusted with hard and soft corals and is gradually becoming part of the reef that caused it to sink. At between 30 m and 70 m it makes an interesting dive, but only for experienced divers; the schools of barracuda add to the interest.

Chrisoula K was a 106 m Greek cargo ship carrying Italian tiles that struck Shab Abu Nuas reef at full speed. The wreck remains upright but at an angle with the bow nearer the surface. The hull and much of the superstructure can be visited with safety but the badly damaged bow section should be avoided in rough weather.

Other wrecks include two off El-Quseir, at Brothers Islands, and a 4000-tonne British steamer between Golbal Island and Tawila. Hurghada port has its own wreck, an Egyptian minesweeper sunk in 1973; it is at a depth of 28 m.

www.cameldive.com. One of the longest established dive centres in Na'ama, slick and friendly service with a 3.5-m training pool. Popular bar inside the dive club area and internet café. Appeals to young cosmopolitan crowd. There is a hotel with 38 rooms in the dive club – comfortable and convenient if you're here to dive, but not cheap. Lots of daily dive trips. Caters to disabled divers.

Emperor Divers, at the Rosetta Hotel on Peace Rd, T069-360 1734, www.emperor divers.com. Highly recommended and known for being sticklers when it comes to safety. A good choice for an open-water course (handy nursery pool) as well as being hugely popular with experienced divers. Offers free transport to/from any hotel, and also organizes live-aboards. Has several branches covering the Sinai and Red Sea coasts.

Mr Diver, T069-360 3796, www.mister diver.com. A reputable outfit, with offices in the Marriott in Na'ama and the Pyramisa in Shark's Bay, popular with Italians, competitively priced.

Oonas Dive Club, at the far northern end of Na'ama Bay, T069-360 1501, www.oonas diveclub.com. Mainly European instructors and divers. Pretty much the cheapest for PADI courses, unusual in that 1st dives are actually in the sea in a buoyed-off area. Overseas bookings that include flights can be made online. Mention your *Footprint Handbook* to receive a 10% discount.

Red Sea Diving College, Sultana Building, on the beachfront, T069-360 0145, www.redseacollege.com. PADI 5-star fully equipped IDC centre. Opened 1991, at least 10 multilingual PADI instructors from a good purpose-built facility. Like **Oonas**, it's one of the cheaper and more reputable places to take a dive course.

Sinai Divers, in Ghazala Hotel, www.sinai divers.com. Claims to be the largest diving centre in Na'ama Bay, certainly one of the most established. Germans and Brits make up a large part of their clientele. Book in advance in the winter high season. Consistently runs week-long live-aboard boats of a high spec, in addition to lots of daily dive trips and the full range of PADI-certified courses (around €350). They also have branches in Dahab, Taba and Marsa Alam.

Live-aboards Live-aboards are boats that offer accommodation and diving on week-long expeditions. There is a huge variety of boats to choose from, ranging from the tolerable to the luxurious. They sleep anything from 8 to 20 people and all include a dive instructor, dive master and cook. The main advantage of live-aboards is that they cover all the same dive sites as the daily boats but tend to hit them at different times, which means a lot less people in the water and a more intimate diving experience. Another advantage is that divers need not swim very far to dive because the boat is already above the site. A few days offshore also gives divers an opportunity to travel to more remote sites like the waters around Gubal Island. Most visitors to Sharm book a live-aboard in advance with a tour company from their home country but it's also possible to book with a local diving centre. Booking ahead is advisable as these boats tend to fill up fast and have very specific departure/arrival times. Individual travellers should enquire with specific diving centres to find a suitable safari.

Dive sites Against all the odds of decades past, Ras Mohammed and the surrounding reefs are still among the world's top dive sites. The diving opportunities around Sharm are so varied and rich, you'd need a book to highlight them all. The guide that most local dive masters use is Alberto Siliotti's *Sharm El-Sheikh Diving Guide*, which is available in dive shops.

The following is a list of some key sites:

Amphoras/Mercury Unnamed Turkish wreck with a cargo of mercury still evident, on the sandy floor at 25 m. This is a relatively easy dive.

Na'ama Bay Despite the incessant construction and traffic, Na'ama is still teeming with life. There's great snorkelling right off the shore and a lot of people do their introductory dive courses here where shore diving is still possible.

Ras Nasrani A dramatic reef wall dotted with caves. There are 2 spots worthy of note: **The Light**, a 40-m drop-off, with large pelagic fish; and **The Point**, with hard coral boulders. Be mindful of the currents.

Ras Umm Sidd Local site in front of the light tower, within walking distance from Sharm El-Sheikh, abundant with soft corals and fan corals. In summer, with the colliding currents, there is an abundance of pelagics (ocean-going fish) passing.

Shark Bay About 10 km north of Na'ama Bay, this site offers a smooth slope shore entry. It's ideal for beginners and 1st-time

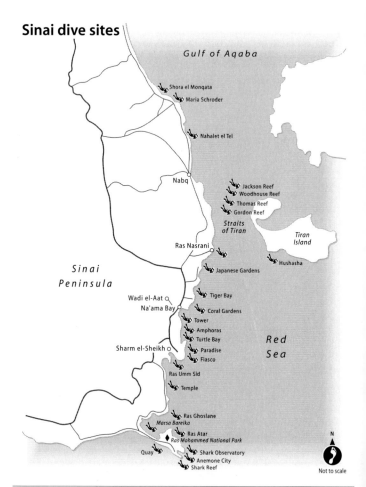

Sinai dive sites

Gulf of Aqaba

Shora el Monqata
Maria Schroder

Nahalet el Tel

Nabq

Jackson Reef
Woodhouse Reef
Thomas Reef
Gordon Reef

Straits of Tiran

Tiran Island

Ras Nasrani

Hushasha

Sinai Peninsula

Japanese Gardens

Tiger Bay

Wadi el-Aat
Na'ama Bay

Coral Gardens

Tower
Amphoras
Turtle Bay
Paradise
Fiasco

Sharm el-Sheikh

Red Sea

Ras Umm Sld

Temple

Ras Ghoslane
Marsa Bareika
Ras Atar
Ras Mohammed National Park

Quay

Shark Observatory
Anemone City
Shark Reef

N

Not to scale

night divers. There's a good restaurant, dive centre and simple accommodation. The dive site has a reputation for manta rays.

Ras Mohammed In efforts to preserve this pristine marine garden that offers some of the best snorkelling and diving in the world, access to some areas is restricted and there are limits on the number of boats that can approach. The sheer volume of soft corals, of incredible shapes and colours, are worth the trip in itself. Of the 20 dive sites in the park, **Shark Reef** is worthy of note. Hanging on the southernmost tip of the Sinai Peninsula, currents split along the site resulting in a hugely varied spectacle of life. Depending on the season, you'll see whatever you could see in the Red Sea: sharks, turtles, thousands of schools of fish, a wonderland. **Yolanda**, another popular dive site in Ras Mohammed, is a sea-bottomed wreck from the early 1980s that resulted in countless toilets sprawled around the ocean floor. It is nothing short of surreal to wander amid the wonders of the sea and a bunch of porcelain toilets.

Straits of Tiran Popular with more experienced divers, the straits of Tiran include **Jackson**, **Woodhouse**, **Thomas** and **Gordon** reefs. There are fantastical coral walls, both of hard and soft coral, extremely lively with fish, while in the deeper waters the chance of seeing a dolphin pod is high. The currents can be strong so this area is not advisable for novices. The residue of a few wrecks including *Sangria* and *Laura* are scattered about the strait. Sharks are common. Jackson reef has a 70-m drop-off. There are also coral reefs at 10-15 m, with many large pelagic fish. **Hushasha**, southwest off the island of Tiran is shallow with a sandy floor and sea grass.

The Tower Steep wall, 60 m, large caves with colourful array of fish. The Tower has been so over-dived in recent years that the spot has lost some of its old splendour, but the wall and colours are still impressive.

Go-karts
Ghibli Raceway, near the Hyatt Regency on the road to the airport, T069-360 3939, www.ghibliraceway.com. It's really fun and really expensive. US$20-35 buys you 10 mins on the track, open 1200-0100.

Horse riding
Sofitel, T069-360 0081. Has good stables and relatively healthy horses that can be hired per hour or per day. They also offer overnight desert trips on horseback.

Ice-skating
Soho Square, near the airport, has a fair-sized ice-rink where a session costs E£90.

Motorcycles and quad bikes
Although you can't hire a motorbike to get about town, you can play on a track with **Sahara Express**, info@ktmegypt.com, behind the Marriott on the far side of Peace Rd. They also have quad bikes, as do **Sun N Fun**, T069-360 1623, www.sunnfunsinai.com where they can be rented by the hour (about US$35) or for short desert rides (accompaniment by a local is a legal requirement).

Snorkelling
A cheaper, easier, and less bulky way to enjoy the magic of the sea is by hiring or investing in a snorkel. Equipment can be rented at diving centres and purchased in many beachfront stores. For more remote snorkelling spots, **The Coral Gardens** north of Na'ama Bay, are accessed from the main Peace highway. Look for easy entry into the water so you won't have to splice your feet and kill the coral on your way in. Access is significantly easier during high tide. In the shallows, you will find a vast array of wondrous creatures, corals that open and close, fish that kiss your goggles, exquisite rainbow colours and patterns. Nearby **Ras Um Sidd** is another exquisite place to mill out in

the blue with its extreme and diverse drop-offs where currents collide and bring in a wide array of fish. **Ras Mohammed**, too, is a splendid place to snorkel with warm waters and sheltered coves offering homes to over 1000 different kinds of sea life. Check weather conditions carefully before tagging onto a dive boat, as choppy seas and strong currents can make the experience risky, and there is unlikely to be any supervision.

Tour operators
There are travel agents attached to almost all the major hotels, as well as independent ones that can book transport, hotels, sightseeing, desert trips and other excursions. Some better known and reputable agents are:
Spring Tours, Hadaba, T069-366 4427, www.springtours.com.
Sun N Fun, Na'ama Bay, T069-360 1623, www.sunnfunsinai.com.
Thomas Cook, in Gafy Mall (Peace Rd) Na'ama Bay, T069-360 1808. Helpful with travel arrangements to other cities, reserves tickets on the ferry to Hurghada.
Travco, Banks Rd, Hadaba, T069-366 0764, www.travco.com. One of Egypt's biggest agents, offering a wide range of day trips throughout Sinai.

Water sports
In addition to snorkelling and diving, there are countless other ways to enjoy the sea. Glass-bottom boats are offered from most hotels along Na'ama Bay's boardwalk, and there are trips to nearby coral reefs (a popular destination is Tiran Island; snorkelling in the lagoon is a must). You can also rent windsurf boards, hobicats and masks and fins. **Colona watersports**, at the Regency Plaza Resort in Nabq, www.colonawatersports.com, offer kiteboarding, and in 4 days you can become a qualified IKO Level II kiteboarder. Jet skis were banned in Sharm a few years back when 2 Italian tourists died as a result of another tourist's carelessness.

Dahab p38, map p39

Desert safaris
Dahab is a good place to set off for the interior by camel or jeep. You can venture inland on a camel with a Bedouin for a few hours, enjoy a cup of tea, and come back to civilization, or you can go for days or weeks at a time to trek around the Sinai, explore the surrounding oases, and dine under diamond-studded skies on coal-cooked grub and fresh Bedouin bread. Like most things, the going rate varies depending on the season, but expect to pay about E£40 per hr for a camel ride and about E£50 per hr for a horse led by a beach-wandering guide. For day-long safaris with food included, it's E£300 or more per day. Popular destinations on camel include **Wadi Gnay** a nearby oasis with a few palms and a brackish spring; **Nabq**, inbetween Dahab and Sharm, a protectorate area that offers the largest mangrove forest in Sinai (see page 37). By jeep, for E£200 per person, you can see the **Coloured Canyon**, a beautiful rift with spectacular rock formations covered with swirls and streaks of countless shades of pink, silver, orange and even gold. The trip generally includes the hr-long trek down the canyon. Due to its increasing popularity, be forewarned that it can be quite crowded. Note that from Nuweiba there is cheaper and easier access. **The White Canyon**, often included on day-long jeep trips with the Coloured Canyon, has cloud-white smooth rocks you can hike up. Virtually all the camps and large hotels can either organize the short safaris to nearby attractions or point you in the right direction. Overnight trips and more extensive safaris cost around E£380 per day. The following are a few notable safari companies based in Dahab that may be bit more expensive, but are safe, experienced and well equipped to organize long-distance journeys into remote areas.
Best Friends Safari, T018-298 9716, www.bestfriendssafari.com. The owner,

Ahmed, is a vibrant, friendly man who knows the desert well and has worked with local Bedouin for years. He will help you create the trip you want.

Embah Safari, near the Lighthouse, Masbat, T069-364 1690, www.embah.com. Committed to eco-tourism and employing local Bedouin expertise, Embah provide tailor-made excursions for days or weeks at a time and offer educational, adventure, marine and desert safaris. An extremely professional, safe and respectable choice. Also have daily departures, booking ahead is advisable.

Nomad Safari, on the promenade, Mashraba, www.nomadsafarisinai.com. Trips to all around South Sinai and further, with emphasis on Bedouin experiences. Also offer rock-climbing.

Diving

Some of the best diving in Dahab is accessible by land. There are more than 40 diving centres in and around Assalah that rent equipment and run PADI diving courses. Not all are considered to be safe. Accidents used to occur on a daily basis and every year there were a number of deaths. Standards have improved of late, but ask around before choosing a dive centre and ensure whoever you choose to study or dive with is PADI certified, reputable and experienced. See also the box on responsible diving on page 53.

There are many stunningly beautiful and interesting dive sites close to Dahab that are generally less crowded than Sharm El-Sheikh and Hurghada, and since most are shore dives, they don't require the added expense of a boat, which keeps the prices down a bit and allows greater flexibility as divers are not tied to the departure times of boats. The downside is that everything you will see is on a smaller scale, including the marine life. Following is a list of recommended centres, but remember that managers and instructors do change and with them so may the quality of the centre. Prices range from €40-60 for 1 day's diving

with full equipment. PADI Open Water courses are in the region of €250-300, plus €30 for the manual. Some dive centres don't include the US$30 certificate fee in the cost of the course so enquire. Most of the centres have instructors catering for a number of languages, including English, French and German.

Big Blue, Assalah, T069-364 0045, www.bigbluedahab.com. Well-regarded operation, provides underwater camera for use on last day of the PADI course.

Desert Divers, Masbat, T069-364 0500, www.desert-divers.com. The only Bedouin-owned dive operation in Dahab, long-established and recommended. Also offers freediving and camel/diving safaris, which trek through rugged lands to reach isolated dive spots.

Fantasea, at the northern end of Masbat bay, near the lighthouse, T069-364 1195, www.fantaseadiving.net. Also rent out windsurf boards.

Inmo, Inmo Hotel and Dive Centre, T069-364 0370-1, www.inmodivers.de. Established since 1988, people keep coming back here.

Nesima, Nesima Hotel, Mashraba, T069-3640 0320, www.nesima-resort.com. Reputable dive centre.

Penguin, Mashraba, T069-364 0117, www.penguindivers.com. Has some very cheap on-the-spot offers on PADI courses (€180 plus €32 for manual) and day dives (€18).

Poseidon Divers, Crazy Camel Camp, Peace Rd, Mashraba, T069-364 0091, www.poseidondivers.com.

Red Sea Research, www.redsea research.org. This non-profit enterprise teaches skills used in marine research projects (eg gathering data, conservation techniques), geared towards gap year or marine science students.

Reef 2000, Bedouin Moon Hotel, between Dahab and Blue Hole, T069-364 0087, www.reef2000.org. Catering mainly for the British and German markets. Offers camel safari to Ras Abu Ghallum, includes food and 2 dives, €100.

Dive sites

North from the lighthouse:

Eel Garden A 15-min walk north of lighthouse, off Assalah, the shallow coral reef is especially good for snorkelling and a safe spot for beginner divers. There's a sandy bottom with a garden of eels, swaying like flowers in the currents as they wait for fish. However, for half the year the currents and winds make diving impossible here – this gives the coral an important break.

The Canyon Opposite **Canyon Dive Centre** a few kilometres north of Dahab. Accessible from the shore, you snorkel along the reef through a narrow break before diving into the canyon. A popular spot for more experienced divers, it bottoms out at 50 m.

The Blue Hole 7 km north of Dahab, the most famous – and infamous – dive in the area. The hole is over 80 m deep and just a few metres from the shore. About 60 m down, there's an arched passageway to the other side of the hole. Attempting to go through it is strongly discouraged. Every year there are stories of advanced divers who die from nitrogen narcosis or carelessness while attempting this dive. At 60 m, you can't see anything anyway, the majesty and life of the place is closer to the surface. Be advised that the Blue Hole is difficult, dangerous and only for very experienced divers.

The Bells Just north of the Blue Hole, along a coral cliff that leads to the hole. A good place to snorkel. Rich with coral and large fish. South from the lighthouse:

The Islands An enchanting and pristine site just south of Dahab near the Laguna. Close to town and easily accessible from shore. Offers multiple routes in a maze of pathways through delicate pinnacles of coral and rainbow-coloured fish. Light and bright, the experience is a hazy and surreal dream.

A bit further out than the aforementioned sites lies **Ras Abu Gallum** (see page 63), a majestic and remote protectorate area that shelters some of the richest marine life in Sinai. Beginning about 15 km north of Dahab, this stretch of 30 km is only accessible by camel. There are 3 main dive sites with virgin reefs and a wide array of marine life. Most of the listed dive centres lead day-long trips to Ras Abu Galum that include camel transport and 2 dives. Costs range from €60-130 depending on season, number of dives and if you need gear.

Some dive centres in Dahab lead trips to the *Thistlegorm*. Enquire at **Inmo** or **Fantasea** (see page 59).

Kitesurfing and windsurfing

A consistently strong and steady breeze makes Dahab among the top places to windsurf in Sinai. Several of the high-end hotels, including the **Hilton** and the **Coralia** with its perfect private windsurfing beach, offer surfing schools with introductory classes up to 3-day courses. In Assalah, **Fantasea Dive Centre** rents boards.

Quad bikes

A few places offer quad biking, try **RAM**, on the main road in Mashraba, T012-700 8017, AymanBassyouny@hotmail.com, who offer trips for around E£150-200 for 2 hrs or **Sinai Experts**, in the Hilton hotel.

Snorkelling

Amazing opportunities for snorkelling abound right off the coast of Assalah. Though a coral reef follows the rim of the entire bay, the best spots are right in front of the lighthouse and further south along the reefs of Mashraba. Be aware that despite the reef's proximity to the shore, the currents can be very strong. All the sites listed under Diving are excellent snorkelling areas, particularly popular are **Ras Abu Gallum**, the **Eel Garden** and the **Blue Hole**. All dive centres in Dahab rent snorkel, mask and fins for around E£30 per day. You can also rent them directly at the Blue Hole.

⊕ Transport

Sharm El-Sheikh *p33, map p34*

Air
Sharm El-Sheikh International Airport, T069-362 3304/5, is 10 km north of Na'ama Bay with direct flights to and from an increasing number of European cities. Most European charter flights and British Airways leave from the newer Terminal 1 while British charter flights leave from Terminal 2, but check as it's a 5- to 10-min walk between the 2. At least 2 internal flights daily with EgyptAir to **Cairo**, 3 per week to **Hurghada**, 4 per week to **Luxor**, and 4 per week to **Alexandria**.

Airline offices EgyptAir, Sharm Old Market, open 0900-2100, T069-366 1058; www.egyptair.com.

Bus
The **East Delta** bus station, T069-366 0660, has recently relocated to Hay El-Nour, halfway between Hadaba and Na'ama Bay. Microbuses aren't direct from Habada/Old Sharm/Na'ama, you will have to change on Peace Rd by the Mobil petrol station. At least 12 buses daily to **Cairo**, running from 0730 in the morning until 0100. Costing E£60-70, the trip is 6-8 hrs. Other destinations include: **Suez** (E£30-35, 5-6 hrs); **Dahab**, at 0900, 1430 and 1700 (E£12, 1½ hrs), of which the 0900 and 1700 go on to **Nuweiba** (E£25, 2½ hrs) and the 1030 carries on to **Taba** (E£35, 3½ hrs). **East Delta** also run 1 bus daily to **Luxor** at 1800 (E£100, 12-14 hrs) and **Alexandria** at 0900 (E£90, 9 hrs). As the schedules are constantly changing, it's best to check departure times. **Superjet** T069-366 1622, have slightly more comfortable buses with toilets, 7 per day to **Cairo** between 1030 and 2330 (E£70) one of which carries on to

Alexandria at 1500 (E£90). **Cairo** is also served by **Go Bus** on Peace Road opposite Delta Sharm Resort.

Car hire
Shahd Limosine, Kalila Centre, Na'ama Bay, T069-360 3066.
Note Drivers beware: there is only 1 petrol station on the 81-km route between Dahab and Sharm El-Sheikh.

Sea
Ferry To **Hurghada**, T069-360 0936, T012-636 0094, 5 per week on Sat, Mon, Tue and Thu at 1700 and Wed at 1800 (from Hurghada to **Sharm El-Sheikh**, same days at 0930, or 0430 on Wed), takes 2 hrs, costs about E£250/US$45, 1 way, E£450 return. To secure a spot, make reservations a day in advance at a hotel or private travel agent like **Thomas Cook**, T069-360 1808. Ferry leaves from the Sharm marina, T069-366 0313.
Private vessels Visas may be obtained for boats and crews from Egyptian consulates in country of origin. It is possible but more hassle to get one in Sharm El-Sheikh. It is as well to give clear advance (at least 1 week) notification of your intention to berth in the port. The Port Commander must be notified upon arrival. The course of the vessel, in national waters, must be filed and approved by the Port Authority.

Dahab *p38, map p39*

Bus
The **East Delta** bus station, T069-364 1808, is on the northern side of Dahab City. There are 4 daily buses to **Cairo** at 0900, 1230, 1500 and 2200 (E£90, 8-9 hrs) via **Sharm El-Sheikh** (E£11-16, 1½ hrs), plus a further 8 buses go to Sharm between 0800-2230. 2 buses go north to **Nuweiba** at 1030 and 1830 (E£11, 1 hr) of which the 1030 carries on to **Taba** (E£25, 3 hrs) and will drop you off at beach camps on the way. 2 buses go to

Ismailia at 1000 and 2230. There's a gruelling bus to **Luxor** every day at 1600 (E£120, 14-15 hrs) which also stops at **Hurghada**. For **St Catherine's** you will have to join a minibus tour from Dahab (E£80-100, departs 2300), or for a drop-off in St Catherine's it's E£60 if you haggle. Bus schedules are posted around most camps. Overnight buses tend to be more expensive.

Car hire
Can be arranged at the **Dahab Hilton**.

Taxi
Service taxis Faster than the bus, another way to get around from city to city is to wait a service (pronounced *servees*) taxi, which leave when full from next to the bus station.
Taxis A necessary expense for getting between Dahab City and the beaches. Tourists are usually charged more than Egyptians. To and from the bus station costs E£5. If you join others or take a pickups it's cheaper. To the Blue Hole, E£50 – the driver will wait and bring you back. If you are travelling en masse or can team up with some other wanderers, it is also a good way to get to St Catherine's or other places further afield.

⊙ Directory

Sharm El-Sheikh *p33, map p34*
Medical services Sharm El-Sheikh International Hospital, 24-hr emergency room, T069-366 0984, midway between Sharm and Na'ama Bay, looks like a pyramid. **Hyperbaric Centre**, at the Travco Marina in Sharm El-Maya, T069-366 0922, for decompression emergencies T012-212 4292. **South Sinai Hospital**, Kennedy Mall, Peace Rd, T069-920 5790/4, T012-000 3533/44, open 24 hrs. For non-emergency cases, **Sharm Medical Centre** on Peace Rd, T069-366 1744, or there are doctors on call at the larger hotels. There are vast numbers of pharmacies, clearly signed, all over Sharm and Na'ama and larger hotels have them on site.

East coast north of Dahab

As the Gulf of Aqaba narrows, sprawling coastal resorts are replaced by intimate camps and the mountains of Saudi Arabia loom ever closer across the tranquil sea. Nuweiba, from where ferries leave for Jordan, has plenty of mellow places that provide a real escape from humanity while still having all amenities to hand. Venturing further north, civilization peters out and simple Bedouin getaways mingle with the occasional tourist village along a dazzling stretch of coast. The road leads to the border town of Taba, in Egyptian hands since 1989, and chiefly of interest as an entry point to Israel.

Ras Abu Gallum

Getting there From the Blue Hole, you can hire a camel (E£80) for the hour's journey along a magical track skirting the coast. You can also walk from the Blue Hole (bear in mind there is no shade), or simply arrange a car-and-camel trip in advance from Dahab. It is also possible to arrive from Nuweiba, to the north, by 4WD, which takes nearly two hours. The first 30 minutes, from Nuweiba to the sizeable Bedouin village of Bir Zehir, is on paved road, but after that the track is rough and corrugated.

In addition to the pristine marine gardens at Ras Abu Gallum, another protectorate area designated in 1992, the coast between Dahab and Nuweiba holds some of the most striking above-ground scenery in Sinai. High mountains and long winding valleys run right down to the sea. Although the Protectorate is valued mainly for its rare plant life, the diving here is also superb. It should be noted, however, that access to the underwater cave network at Ras Mamlah is strictly forbidden. Many divers have died here and their bodies remain unrecovered.

Most people come to dive, but the snorkelling along the reef is some of Sinai's best (bring equipment). Ras Abu Gallum remains a majestic tranquil spot with a welcoming Bedouin community and glorious beaches, but it is not unspoiled by the camel trains of tourists trudging through. Lying on the very edge of the sea, the Bedouin village itself is rather scruffy and made largely from plywood. There are several huts on the beach where you can stay, a shop, a couple of restaurants and tea-shops. There is also a solar-powered information centre, plus plenty of bright-eyed Bedouin children who will ask you to buy their jewellery. However, to find complete peace and magic you only have to go a couple of kilometres further north to the **Blue Lagoon** (45 minutes' walk, note that there is another little Bedouin encampment between Ras and the Lagoon). There, the most perfectly aquamarine sea filters into a lagoon set off by blindingly white sand and a reef lies just offshore (with excellent snorkelling when the sea is calm). A couple of idyllic camps await (see Where to stay, page 67).

Nuweiba → *For listings, see pages 67-72.*

Nuweiba lies 67 km north of Dahab and 64 km south of the Israeli border at Taba on a dazzlingly beautiful stretch of coast. Nuweiba's 'moshav', or cooperative village, used to be a major destination for Israeli tourists during the occupation but has long since been surpassed by Na'ama Bay as the Sinai's primary resort destination. The diving here might be rather tame in comparison to Sharm, but Nuweiba has many splendid sandy beaches with comfortable hotels that tend to be cheaper and are in closer proximity to Israel, Jordan and the wonders of the desert interior.

The town is divided into three distinct areas: the 'city', the port to the south, and the Bedouin village of Tarabeen to the north. Sadly, all three areas (and indeed many of the hotels and small camps along the coast up to Taba) have an eerie ghost-town feel since the second Intifada and, at the time of writing, continued tension means Israeli tourists are conspicuously absent from all but the camps closest to the border. Neglect is much in evidence, as the skeletons of unfinished bungalows and old bamboo huts disintegrate and plastic bags wash up on stretches of Nuweiba's gorgeous coast. But if complete peace and freedom from hassle are what you desire, there are still plenty of cosy camps on clean white sand to be found, and Nuweiba has a natural advantage over most of Dahab in that you can swim straight off the beach and snorkel out to some colourful reefs. Aside from winding down and floating in the Red Sea, it is also a much better place to get to meet Bedouin people and give something back to Sinai by organizing a tailor-made trip into the interior in the company of some locals to see the spectacular wadis and mountain villages.

Arriving in Nuweiba

Getting around Nuweiba port is the set-off point for the ferry across the gulf to Aqaba. All the buses arrive at Nuweiba port and some continue on to the town centre or vice versa. You can ask the bus driver to drop you off at your chosen camp along the coast north of Nuweiba. From the port you can take a taxi that will deliver you directly to town or the village. Taxis in these parts have an unspoken camaraderie and tend to charge foreigners inflated prices for transport. Standard fare from the port to town centre is E£10-20, from the port to Tarabeen, E£20-30, and from Tarabeen to the town centre E£10. Any jeep or pickup cruising past will offer you 'taxi' and prices become more negotiable. Bargain hard and keep a sense of humour.
▶▶ See Transport, page 72.

Places in Nuweiba

Lounging on the beach, swimming and snorkelling, and playing backgammon, billiards or dominoes are about all one does in Nuweiba itself. The wild dolphin, Oleen, which befriended Abdullah, a local deaf

Nuweiba

To Taba

TARABEEN

Gulf of Aqaba

Tourist
Bazaar

Bedouin
Cultural Safaris

Duty Free
Shop

Port
To Aqaba

To Dahab

N

Not to scale

Nuweiba Hilton
Coral Village 2
Nuweiba Village 6
Petra Camp 7
Sababa Camp 8
Waha Village 10

Where to stay
Blue Bus 1
La Sirene 4
Mondial Village 3
Nakhil Inn 5
New Soft Beach 9

Restaurants
Cleopatra 1
Dr Shishkabab 3
Habiba 2
Han Kang 4

Bedouin, and became a rather dubious tourist attraction for a while, is no longer seen these days. There are plenty of enterprising local Bedouin who organize camel treks and jeep safaris into the magnificent interior for day trips and more extensive overnight safaris. Many visitors also make short trips to Petra in Jordan via the ferry to Aqaba.

Tarabeen

A 20-minute walk along the beach north of Nuweiba city lies the Bedouin settlement of Tarabeen, sprawled along a stunningly beautiful bay. Reminiscent of Dahab a decade back, there are traditional 'camps', Bedouin-style restaurants and a couple of hotels scattered about a dirt road alongside mini bazaars where shopping is relaxed and easy. However, since the outbreak of the first Intifada in late September 2000, Israelis, who made up over 80% of the tourism around Nuweiba, have virtually stopped coming. As a result, several camps and restaurants have closed, trash is washing up on the shores, and there is a tangible air of sadness in parts. Yet many camps are keeping standards up while the authorities are have recently been trying to smarten the beachfront up, and it's easy to fall in love with the place. From the shore you can see the mountains of Saudi Arabia painted pink on the near horizon as the Gulf of Aqaba narrows towards the north, and as night falls tiny clusters of lights come on in villages across the water – it is utterly magical.

Nuweiba to Taba

Along the striking stretch of shore between Nuweiba and Taba where rugged red mountains twist and turn and pour down to the sea, there are several scatterings of Bedouin camps and tourist villages that offer respite and serenity away from the more trafficky resorts of the south. They all are accessible via bus or service taxi; simply ask the driver to drop you by the roadside at your desired destination. Some camps are dilapidated forgone attempts falling apart at the seams, others are gems and sensitive to their environs. Notable is **Ras Al-Shaitan**, which means 'Devil's Head', an area named for a peculiar rock formation by the beach, 12 km north of Nuweiba. Here, a string of camps on the beach under an amazing virgin Sinai sky are kept busy by Israeli tourists, and there is excellent snorkelling just 20 m offshore. A downside is that the beach is stony in comparison to other places. **Basata**, meaning 'simplicity' in Arabic, is 23 km north of Nuweiba and the eco-lodge here is one of Sinai's most popular get-aways for good reason – the beach is divine and ambiance perfect. Three kilometres north of Basata and 30 km south of Taba is **Bir Sweir**, where a 2-km-long swathe of soft sandy beach has numerous cheap camps all offering decent facilities (due to its popularity with young Israelis), a reef excellent for snorkelling, and the sun sets on the mountains of Saudi Arabia turning the sea pink. **Taba Heights**, a tourist development just 9 km southwest of Taba, is a newly built 'resort village' comprising of hotels, restaurants, shops and a marina attracting European visitors directly to Taba airport 20 km away. To date, several huge high-end hotels with hundreds of rooms have been built and enjoy 5 km of beach, pools, health clubs, a golf course, casinos and all other five-star amenities, with more luxury hotels under construction. There is a good watersports centre here, whose diving, windsurfing, canoes, etc can be used by travellers who are staying at the smaller camps to the south.

Taba tug of war

Taba is an enclave of land of no more than 1 sq km on the Gulf of Aqaba seized by the Israelis in the war of 1956 but, unlike the rest of Sinai, not returned to Egypt. Assuming that the Taba strip would be forever Israeli, an international hotel complex was built there (now the Taba Hilton). In 1986 agitation by Egypt for a final settlement of the international border at Taba led the dispute being put to arbitration.

This revealed that the border post at Ras Taba, one of 14 put in place after the 1906 Anglo-Turkish agreement, had been moved by the Israeli side.

In one of the oddest of cases concerning the delimitation of an international border, it was found that the Israeli army had cut away part of the hill at Ras Taba to enable Israeli artillery to have a good sweep of the Sinai coast road as it approached the port of Eilat. At the same time the Israeli military engineers removed the border post that rested on the top of Ras Taba. This gave the Israeli government the excuse to claim that, despite Israeli maps to the contrary, the old border had always run south of the Taba strip. In 1989 the arbitrators returned Taba to Egypt, though it remains virtually an enclave with border posts on all sides.

Taba → *For listings, see pages 67-72.*

This town has a special place in the hearts of most Egyptians because, although it is only tiny, it was the last piece of territory that was occupied by the Israelis. The fact that the luxury Sonesta hotel, one of Israel's best and most popular hotels, was in the Taba enclave no doubt complicated the dispute. Despite having to pay compensation to the Sonesta's owners, before handing the hotel over to the Hilton group to manage and despite the very small size of the area in dispute, Cairo had been determined to retrieve every centimetre of Egyptian land and was satisfied by the outcome.

Taba is unusual, an international border town between an empty desert and the bright lights of Eilat. The coastline is beautiful but exceedingly windy. Besides hotels there is little else in the tiny enclave except barracks and facilities for the border guards and customs officials. Having won Taba back from Israel, the government is now concentrating on development of the tourist industry in the region and is building power stations and other infrastructural facilities to support the planned influx.

Arriving in Taba

Getting there and around   The easiest way to reach Taba, 390 km from Cairo and 260 km from Sharm El-Sheikh, is via the airport, which has both domestic and international charter flights. Some tourists arrive via Israel's Eilat airport, which is only 15 km across the border. Guests of the Taba Hilton and Nelson Village, see page 70, do not have to pay Israeli departure tax. These hotels will provide a pass to allow free movement through the border during your time of stay.

Places in Taba

Sightseeing in Taba is limited to visits across the Israeli border to Eilat, trips to the beautiful interior, or boats to **Pharaoh's Island**, where lie the ruins of Salah Al-Din's fortress (the most important Islamic remains in Sinai). The fortress was originally built in 1115 by the Crusaders to guard the head of the Gulf of Aqaba and protect pilgrims travelling between Jerusalem and St Catherine's monastery. It was also used to levy taxes on Arab merchants travelling to and from Aqaba. Salah Al-Din took it over in 1171 but abandoned it in the face of European attacks 12 years later. The island is a short boat ride (400 m) from the Salah-el-Din Hotel and the hotel also organizes snorkelling trips around the island's surrounding reefs, but beware – the currents can be strong.

Taba Managed Resource Protected Area is the newest and largest in the network of coastal and inland protected areas (designated in January 1998). It lies south and west of Taba and includes the Coloured Canyon. There is a wealth of ancient writings and carvings on rock walls in the area that span the history of Sinai, the crossroads between Asia and Africa. The scripts include Arabic, Semitic, Greek, Nabatean and other, unknown, languages.

◉ East coast north of Dahab listings

For sleeping and eating price codes and other relevant information, see pages 11-15.

● Where to stay

Ras Abu Gallum and the Blue Lagoon
p63
In the Bedouin village at Ras Abu Gallum there are about 10 modest huts on the beach right next to the sea that can be rented for E£20 per person per night. There are a few squat toilets, but no running water or electricity. Water and other basic necessities are available at inflated prices and there are a couple of restaurants/tea-shops.

At the **Blue Lagoon** there are a couple of small camps, with *hooshas* (huts) that are a step above those at Ras Abu Gallum, with rag-rugs, palm trunk seating areas and good restaurants. But it's the location – quite simply other-worldly in its pristine beauty – that makes the effort of getting here worthwhile:

€€€€ Laguna Camp, has some good huts, a couple of which sit on a spit of land that extends far into the blue waters, while next door **Selim's Camp** nestles by the Bedouin fishing boats on the lagoon. Both places can provide meals (fish E£60).

Nuweiba *p63, map p64*
Nuweiba has a few higher-spec hotels on the shoreline between the town centre and port. There is also a range of comfortable camps and simple hotels in Tarabeen, the most attractive clusters being at the northern and southern points of the beach now that the central area has become rather dilapidated. See also the listings below for a scattering of magical tourist settlements along the coast between Nuweiba and Tarabeen that offer more remote, tranquil accommodation.

€€€€-€€€ Nuweiba Hilton Coral Village, on the beach just north of the port, T069-352 0320, www1.hilton.com. Choice of restaurants, water sports, camel and horse riding, safaris, bicycles, squash, tennis, children's facilities, 2 heated pools, bank, internet access, travel agency, disco. A stylish resort, very relaxing, ideal for recuperating, rather isolated from rest of Sinai resorts. Excellent snorkelling is a 15-min walk away.

Aquasport Dive and Watersport Centre on the beach, one of the best diving centres in Nuweiba.

€€€-€ Helnan Nuweiba, T069-350 0401, www.helnan.com. Cosy chalet-style rooms with all the extras, private beach, dive centre, tennis, beach volleyball, small gym and a sizable pool. It's worth shelling out that bit extra for well-kept grounds, comfy loungers under wicker parasols, and to be somewhere that's fairly bustling (by Nuweiban standards). Half board available. There's also a large cluster of huts.

€€ **La Sirene**, T069-350 0701, www.lasirene hotel.com. Becoming a bit run down, but rooms are spacious with tasteful decor– all have their own balcony and some have a huge rooftop terrace. No pool, but excellent snorkelling on the coral reef, dive centre is open sporadically.

€ **Amon Yahro**, T016-685 2600. Clean huts with attractive seating areas for hanging out, cheap at E£30. Their little patch of beach is very well maintained (around the edges the rubbish is encroaching).

€ **El Waha Village**, T069-350 0420, www.elwahavillage.com. Double rooms in old-fashioned chalets for US$20 (add US$5 for breakfast) with a/c, fridge and TV, or camping on the beach for E£15. It has an air of dereliction, but is kept clean by the pleasant staff.

There's a handful of basic hotels next to the port costing around E£60-90 per night, should you get stranded waiting for the ferry. During the *Hajj* these are always full, but then so is the ferry.

Tarabeen *p65, map p64*

Tarabeen offers a range of possibilities. For E£20, you can still get a hut in one of the basic camps. They are quite comparable in quality, though some have cleaner bathrooms and offer extras like hot water, fans and mosquito nets. For E£50, you can expect to find a room with a/c and private bath.

€€ **Nakhil Inn**, T069-350 0879. A tasteful well-run hotel at the northern tip of the bay, on a spotless private beach with direct access to good snorkelling on the reef (free masks). Rooms are spacious with huge windows (the nicest have a mezzanine with views of the sea from the bed), bar, free Wi-Fi, indoor (with fireplace) and outdoor restaurant, desert excursions, dive centre (closed off-season, but offers trips to Ras Abu Galum when open). Unquestionably the nicest place to stay in Tarabeen. Breakfast included.

€ **Blue Bus**, T010-988 3854, www.blue-bus.de. This camp remains the best laid out in town, with a small cluster of huts (clean linen) nestling by a dune by a sandy stretch of beach, and decked out with cushions and rugs in the chill-out spaces. Doubles E£30.

€ **Mondial Village**, T012-796 3385, mondialvillage@yahoo.com. Stone-built rooms with hot showers en suite, a/c and large clean beds. Food is cheap in a typically laid-back hang-out with a pool table, doubles cost E£50 or E£70 with breakfast, they have beer.

€ **Petra Camp**, T069-350 0086. Run by a young Bedouin lawyer, this place is well-managed and the staff are sweet, offers clean, comfortable huts among a palm garden, decent shared bathrooms with hot water, good food (cheaper than other camps) served as you recline by the water's edge. Guests are consistently happy. Rooms are E£20-40, and there's (slow) internet for E£20 per hr.

€ **Sababa Camp**, T016-183 5517, www.sababacamp.com. An old timer in Tarabeen, huts have doors painted with yin yangs and oms by hippies of yesteryear, as well as fans, mosquito nets, electric outlets and sheets on the beds, bathrooms are clean and the water hot. The restaurant and beach seating is an attractive place to chill out. Desert excursions are offered.

€ **Soft Beach**, T010-364 7586, www.soft beachcamp.com. Managers Kamal and Christine have made the south end of Tarabeen the place to be again. A range of bamboo huts share a good shower block (loo paper), hammocks sway in the breeze and the beach area is swept daily. The reliable menu is a bit pricier, desert trips are easy to arrange – E£200 for 1 person, cost goes down as numbers go up. However, they do get annoyed when you eat your meals at other camps.

Nuweiba to Taba *p65*

Ras Shaitan
€€-€ Castle Beach, next to Ayaash (below), T012-739 8495. A bit more comfortable with tasteful bungalows that have electricity and their own terrace. Sheets and towels can also be provided. The bathrooms are cleaned every few hours, restaurant is excellent but more expensive than most. Desert trips with experienced guides available. Generally busy.

€ Ayaash's Camp (also known simply as 'Ras Shaitan'), T010-525 9109. This is the 1st camp from Nuweiba and lies directly in front of the 'head'. Accommodation is extremely simple, scattered about the hills and shore, some are only a few metres from the waterline. There is no hot water or electricity. Desert safaris are available and it's possible to rent snorkel and fins to explore the reef offshore. There's also a busy restaurant that often is the gathering spot for late-night jam sessions.

€ Seven Heaven, Ras Shaitan, www.seven heavenhotel.com. Friendly family place, of the same dynasty who own places of the same name in Dahab and Luxor. 36 chalets use outside bathrooms, more comfort offered than your basic *hoosha* with beds, mirrors and 2 generators.

Basata
€€-€ Basata Ecolodge, 23 km north of Nuweiba, T069-350 0480/1, www.basata. com. German-educated owner Sherif El-Ghamrawy has created a genuinely environmentally conscious retreat. There is only candlelight in the 18 simple, clean beachfront huts, plus there are 10 domed villas with private bathrooms. Camping is permitted and very popular. There are some

steadfast rules – no drugs or alcohol (in public) and no late-night noise, nudity, or sleeping in the common area. The result is a respectable, family-friendly environment. The kitchen runs on an honour system where guests are invited to take what they want and write it down, but if doing your own cooking doesn't appeal, pizzas and bread are baked fresh daily (minimum charge E£50 per day). Fabulous (optional) communal dinners are served to lodge guests every evening. The beach is perfect and there's a good reef for snorkelling offshore. Sherif organizes desert treks and tours for groups and individuals. It's wise to book ahead, as the huts are often reserved months in advance – especially during national holidays. Israelis will be told it's full, even when it isn't.

Bir Sweir
Breakfasts are not included (usually E£30) and mains are from E£40-80, including the famed *'maglooba'*.

€€ Sally Land Tourist Village, T069-922 0007, www.sallylandresort.com. Tastefully planned khan-like stone chalets with crenulated roofs and domes are pleasantly white and dark wood inside, on a large stretch of beach, though there are few guests unless the German-Egyptian owners have a group booked. Prices are half-board.

€ Alexandria, Bir Sweir, T012-166 1042/ T010-618 7041, www.alexandriabeach.com. The most international of all Bir Sweir's camps, with a mix of Europeans and Israelis plus kindly Sudanese staff, is also one of the largest and most popular. Huts are large with 2-4 beds (E£35 per person), the food is homely, shrubs and colourful rugs adorn the area, and they will get you beer. At the southern end of the beach.

€ Al Tarek, Bir Sweir, T052-635 1449/012-108 1189, www.altarek-sinai.com. About the cutest huts on the beach at Bir Sweir, with curved rush roofs and shady terraces out the front, are laid out with care and thought to privacy. The lovely manager plays Arabic music in the sociable restaurant. E£30 per person.

€ Diana Beach, Bir Sweir, T012-405 0964. Popular place, with good fish meals from the busy kitchen, attractively set out huts and lots of space. Possibly Sinai's best hammock is to be found next to the sea here, E£25 per person.

€ Paradise Sweir, Bir Sweir, T052-500 1622, www.paradisesinai.com. At the northern end of the beach, this is about the cheapest camp at E£15 per person. Scruffy public areas, but the huts are quite sweet, there's a pool table, lots of Israelis and local Bedouin hanging out, generally bustling.

€ Sun Sweir, T018-562 8410. Sweet water showers are a big plus, this smaller camp has 25 huts with lights inside (some with beds, others mattresses). It is open all year round, and especially recommended for the excellent food.

Taba *p66*

The huge resort hotels at **Taba Heights**, which include the **Hyatt**, **Marriott**, **Sofitel** and **Intercontinental**, have all the 5-star trimmings and are chiefly booked from abroad.

€€€€-€€€ Taba Hilton and Nelson Village, T069-353 0140, www.hiltonworld resorts.com. The reliable, high-rise Hilton has dominated the area for years, right on the Israeli border. Private beach looks onto the tip of the Gulf of Aqaba, 2 pools, tennis courts, acceptable restaurants and bars, plus a nightclub and casino. Snorkelling, quad bikes into the desert and trips to Pharaoh's Island are among the activities on offer. **Nelson Village** is an extension of the hotel and they share facilities. It's more sensitively designed using natural materials and set in pleasing gardens.

€€€ Tobya Boutique Hotel, T069-353 0275, www.tobyaboutiquehotel.com. Though it doesn't meet all the credentials of a boutique retreat, it is the most quirky choice in town, 2 km south of the border. It is worth knowing that outside guests can use the 2 pools and private beach for the day, should you be stranded for a few hours in Taba. Prices are half-board.

🍴 Restaurants

Nuweiba *p63, map p64*

€€ Cleopatra, T069-350 0503, in front of Nuweiba Village. Open 0900-2300. Simple fish, meats and salads are freshly prepared and served under flashing fairy lighting.

€€ Dr Shishkabab, in town centre. Open late. Has lost some of its acclaim in recent years but still serves up a cheap shish kabab and other traditional grub; the soups and Egyptian staples are definitely recommended.

€€ Habiba Village, T069-350 0770, www.sinai4you.com/habiba. Open until midnight. Beachside restaurant that cooks up fresh Bedouin bread, good fish, and has an 'Italian Corner'. Can get busy from midday as it caters to tourists on day trips from Sharm enjoying the buffet.

€€ Hang Kang, Mazara Rd, in front of the Helnan hotel. Open 1000-2200. A notable Asian restaurant that has been around for years, serving up surprisingly good Chinese and Korean feasts (mains E£35-75). Hot and sour soup is a winner, plus there are numerous pork dishes, alcohol served.

Tarabeen *p65, map p64*

All the camps and hotels have eating spots bang next to the sea offering similar food at similar prices.

€€ Blue Bus, a popular restaurant with a pleasant beach area to enjoy mid-priced pizzas, pastas and fish. Excellent juices.

€€ Sababa Camp, extensive menu including pizzas, pastas and good fresh fish.

Nuweiba to Taba p65

€€€ Castle Zaman, Taba-Nuweiba Rd, just north of **Basata Ecolodge**, T069-350 1234/018-214 0591, www.castlezaman.com. Open 1200-2230. Set on a hill 1.5 km north of Basata Ecolodge, the owner has spent years perfecting every detail of this dream place, and diners come from afar for the famed slow-cooked meat and seafood specialities, €40 a head (vegetarian version available, but for the same price; book in advance). Alternatively, an entrance charge of E£100 per person allows use of the exquisite pool and private beach for the day, and is redeemable against sunset drinks as the lights start twinkling across the water in the villages of Saudi Arabia. A 'treasure room' has attractive gifts, there's a sauna, and the hilltop setting is divine. Recommended.

Taba p66

€€€ Taba Hilton, has several restaurants serving varying cuisines, all are expensive but of a high standard.

There is a coffee shop in the bazaar opposite the bus station that serves tasty cheap Egyptian staples from about 0600, should you get stranded.

⚠ What to do

Nuweiba p63, map p64

Besides diving and desert safaris, sports equipment and facilities are only available at the large hotels. **The Hilton** rents jetskis and kayaks.

Desert safaris

Desert safaris and excursions are widely available from Nuweiba and the nearby camps and tourist villages. Virtually every hotel and camp has connections with experienced Bedouin that know the desert like the back of their hands. There are countless majestic spots in the Sinai interior, some much more frequented than others.

Most visited is the **Coloured Canyon**, a stunning site even in the midst of tour buses. From Nuweiba, you should be able to find a ride in a jeep for E£150-200. Other striking spots often included on camel and jeep safaris are **Ain Um Ahmed**, a large fertile palm-laden oasis fed by the snowmelts from far-off peaks; the impressive **White Canyon**; and **Wadi Ghazala**, a valley where gazelle are known to graze. Easily accessible in a half-day jeep safari (E£300-350) is **Ain Khudra**, or 'green spring', a magical and tranquil destination where a few families live. There are 3 tea-shops here when travellers can stay overnight, and the setting in a white and gold wadi is memorable.

The cost is fairly consistent – by camel it's E£120 per person for a day safari, E£180 per night, including food. Costs generally do not include water, so plan to bring all you need. For a big adventure, some locals organize camel safaris for 2- to 10-day expeditions into the interiors. Trips might include the mountain plateaux of Gebel El-Guna, passing through little-visited wadis where the wind has carved the coloured sandstone into supernatural forms and awesome white sand dunes startle the eye. If you can't find a Bedouin guide that feels good, **Abanoub Travel**, T069-352 0201, www.abanoub.com, is a reputable tour company that has organized safe camel and jeep safaris for years. They're at the pricier end of the spectrum.

Diving

Nuweiba is known more for sandy beaches than diving, but, because its waters are quiet and clear, it makes a suitable spot for beginners. There are some good snorkelling areas offshore, the most famous is the **Stone House**, just south of town. There are a few dive centres around, all of which offer trips to nearby sites that are more impressive than the few reefs off Nuweiba shores.

SCUBA Divers, based in La Sirene, T069-350 0705. Contact them in advance to check whether an international certified instructor is present on site to teach beginners' courses, as now that Nuweiba is so quiet he's not consistently in town. However, diving and snorkelling gear are always available to rent.

Sinai Diving Centre, at the **Helnan Hotel**, T069-3500 401, www.helnan.com, have a well-maintained and efficient centre in the grounds of the hotel.

⊖ Transport

Nuweiba *p63, map p64*

Bus
T069-520 3701. Departure times from Nuweiba frequently change so ask at any hotel or camp to confirm times. A bus leaves for **Cairo** at 0900 and 1500 (E£70, 7 hrs). **Sharm El-Sheikh** (E£16, 3 hrs) buses go via **Dahab** (E£11, 1 hr) and leave at 0600 and 1600. A bus goes to **Suez** only at 0600 (E£29), or the 0630 for Sharm carries on to Suez though it's much slower. Buses all depart from the terminal at the port. For **St Catherine's**, you must go to Dahab, and arrange transport there.

Microbuses offer cheaper and sometimes quicker transport. They operate on a leave-when-full policy and travel north and south along the main highway as well as to **Cairo**. Check prices before setting off, but you shouldn't pay more than E£70 to go to Cairo.

Ferry
Two ferries to **Jordan** leave from Nuweiba Port at 1400 on Fri-Wed, one is fast and the other slow; on Thu only the slow boat makes the trip. Visas for Jordan are available on board.

Taxis
Service taxis With passengers sharing the cost of the journey, service taxis are available from Nuweiba port to **Taba** and other towns in the region. Taxis around Nuweiba are pricy as it's a captive market – from Tarabeen about E£10 to Nuweiba City and E£20 to the port.

Taba *p66*

Air
Taba Airport, www.taba-heights.co.uk/airport, 18 km inland from Taba, has flights to **Cairo** on Sun and Thu and international charter flights bringing tourists to Taba Heights. There's an **EgyptAir** office in Taba, but it opens sporadically due to lack of demand. **Eilat airport** (15 km from Taba) has direct daily flights to major European cities. (No problem at Egyptian border but customs officials at the airport are very thorough).

Bus
East Delta Bus Co, T069-353 0250, runs daily buses to **Cairo** at 1030 and 1630 (6-7 hrs, E£65), **Sharm El-Sheikh** (4 hrs, E£30) via **Dahab** (3 hrs, E£25) and **Nuweiba** (1 hr, E£11) at 0500 and 1500. There is no direct bus to **St Catherine's**; you have to go to Dahab and join a microbus tour.

Taxis
Service taxis driven by local Bedouin regularly transport visitors to **Nuweiba**, **Dahab** and **Sharm**. They are more frequent, more comfortable, and quicker than buses – but more expensive. Assuming the car is full, expect to pay around E£30 per person to **Tarabeen** and **Nuweiba**, E£50 to **Dahab** and E£80 to **Sharm El-Sheikh**.

The interior

The largest single protected area in Sinai is St Catherine's National Park (designated in 1987), which covers a roughly triangular area of the mountains south from St Catherine's Monastery. This Greek orthodox monastery at the base of Mount Sinai has attracted pilgrims and visitors for centuries and despite its location in the heart of the Sinai wilderness, it's one of the most important tourist sites in the country. The park also contains ibex, gazelle and hyena, hyrax, leopards and possibly cheetahs. It's a relatively untouched region and a safari across the desert plateaux, past dusty acacias and across dry riverbeds, can be done by foot, camel or jeep. A few intrepid trekkers weave between the ragged shards of the high mountains, surprised by the lush gardens hidden in valleys and dazzled by the ochre glow of the landscape against the blue sky. Bedouin have been recruited as guides and community guards to help the rangers patrol this immense expanse of land and noticeable progress is apparent, particularly in clearing the area of rubbish and providing information and nature trails. Another peak nearby (Egypt's highest) with some great hiking potential and a monastery is Mount Catherine and further west is the welcome flash of green that is Wadi Feiran.

St Catherine → *For listings, see pages 78-81.*

Arriving at St Catherine

Getting there The road journey from Dahab to St Catherine, which is generally good with little traffic, takes about 1½ hours. However, there is no public transport so you will have to join a tour or hire a taxi for the journey (about E£180). On the way, at the top of a very steep hill there is a breathtaking view over the desert. The coaches and taxis stop here and Bedouins attempt to sell fossils, sand-roses and other souvenirs. While all of the organized tours to St Catherine stop at the monastery itself, the bus service from Cairo stops in the small village of St Catherine about 2 km from the monastery.

Information St Catherine's National Park visitor centre ① *T069-347 0032, it is supposed to be open Mon-Thu and Sat 0830-1300, but is frequently locked*, is on the main road before the turning to the monastery. Has information on shorter walks, and a few books and maps of the area, and excellent information on the tribes, ecology and history of the region. Alternatively access walking tours and maps online at www.touregypt.net/walkingtours. A useful and inspiring website is www.st-katherine.net, for information on trekking, Bedouin culture and the St Catherine's region in general. The **Tourist Police** ① *T069-347 0046*, are in St Catherine's, main square, opposite the bus station.

Best time to visit St Catherine is very cold in winter with a metre of snow a few times a year, and snow sometimes until March, but it is very hot in summer.

St Catherine's Monastery

① *Cairo office T02-248 28513. Mon-Thu and Sat 0900-1130, Fri 1045-1145, closed Sun and public holidays, free. (Only Orthodox Christians are allowed to attend the long Sun service.) Visitors to the inside of the monastery must dress modestly, no shorts or bare arms are permitted. Although an official tour guide, who will explain the history and symbolism of each part of the monastery, is a bonus he is not essential if you buy the guidebook in the small bookshop near the entrance.*

The **Burning Bush**, through which God is said to have spoken to Moses, holds religious significance for Jews, Christians and Muslims and in AD 337 Empress Helena, mother of Constantine, decreed that a sanctuary was to be built around what was thought to be the site of the bush. This became a refuge for an increasing number of hermits and pilgrims who traversed the wilderness of the Sinai Valley over the following centuries. Israeli pilgrims are few and far between these days, but the monastery has long been unique in that here the three great monotheistic religions have come together peaceably, without clashes. A rather unimpressive overgrown evergreen bush, which is claimed to be a transplanted descendant of the Burning Bush, grows in the courtyard inside the monastery, and there is an almost continual photo-call going on beneath its thorny branches.

Between AD 537 and 562, Emperor Justinian expanded the site considerably by building fortifications and providing soldiers to protect the residents and adding the Church of the Virgin and the Basilica of the Transfiguration. The monastery and its community which then, as today, was controlled by the Byzantine Church were tolerated by the subsequent Muslim conquerors. The number of pilgrims dwindled until a body, claimed to be that of the Egyptian-born St Catherine, was 'discovered' in the 10th century and was brought to the monastery. This attracted many pilgrims during the period of Crusader occupation (1099-1270). The numbers of both pilgrims and monks, who are now restricted to Greeks

St Catherine's Monastery

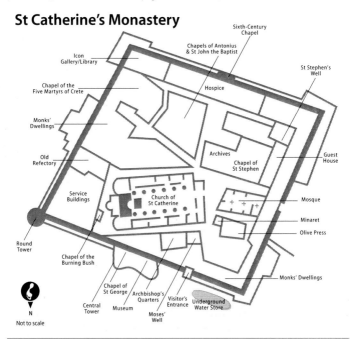

Sixth-Century Chapel

Chapels of Antonius & St John the Baptist

Icon Gallery/Library

St Stephen's Well

Chapel of the Five Martyrs of Crete

Hospice

Monks' Dwellings

Archives

Guest House

Old Refectory

Chapel of St Stephen

Service Buildings

Church of St Catherine

Mosque

Minaret

Olive Press

Round Tower

Monks' Dwellings

Chapel of the Burning Bush

Chapel of St George

Archbishop's Quarters

Visitor's Entrance

Underground Water Store

N

Not to scale

Central Tower

Museum

Moses' Well

mainly from the Mount Athos area, subsequently waxed and waned until today there are only 25 monks, although the thousands of international pilgrims and tourists actually make the monastery unbearably crowded in the high season.

The site The ancient gate on the western face has been walled up (but the funnel above, for pouring oil on unwary attackers, remains) and now visitors enter through a newer door in the north wall. The outer wall, constructed of local granite by Justinian's builders, is 2- to 3-m thick and the height, which varies due to the uneven topography, is never less than 10 m and in places reaches 20 m. The southern face has some interesting raised Christian symbols.

West of the church is a small 11th-century **mosque** which, originally a guesthouse, was converted apparently in order to placate the Muslim invaders and to encourage them to tolerate the monastery. The detached minaret that faces the church is 10 m high. Significantly, however, the church steeple is considerably taller.

Beyond the entrance is the white rectangular minaret of a Fatimid mosque, built in 1106 as a shelter for pilgrims on the way to Mecca, the keys of which are held by the local Jabaliya tribe. On special occasions the mosque is in use, and Bedouins work in the monastery alongside the monks. The highlight of the walled monastery, which includes the monks' quarters, refectory, library and gardens (not open to the public), is the highly decorative and incense-perfumed **Church of the Transfiguration**. The church was built of granite in the shape of a basilica between AD 542-551, in memory of Emperor Justinian's wife. Its 12 enormous pillars, each a single piece of granite, are free-standing and decorated with beautiful icons representing the saints that are venerated in each of the 12 months of the year. A candle is lit below the relevant icon on each saint's day. Examine the capitals for their Christian symbols. The walls, pillars and cedar-wood doors of the church are all original – by comparison, the 11th-century doors made by the Crusaders seem almost new! The ancient roof is hidden above a more recent (18th-century) ceiling with reliefs of animals and plants. Above them the inscription (in Greek) reads, "This is the gate to the Lord; the righteous shall enter into it." The hanging oil lanterns and swinging incense burners, plus Greek monks lit by shafts of sunlight, do something to detract from the camera-wielding masses shuffling through (even though photography is forbidden). The iconostasis is dated at 1612. In the apse is the chief delight of this building – a magnificent mosaic illustrating the Transfiguration. It is the earliest and one of the finest mosaics of the Eastern Church. The theme is taken from St Matthew's Gospel. Christ is in the centre with Moses and Elijah at each side and Peter, James and John at his feet. Around these are further figures identified as the 12 apostles, the 12 prophets, the abbot at the time of the mosaic's construction and John of Climax, the deacon. The three-tiered bell tower at the western end of the church was built in 1871. There are nine bells, each of a different size. They came as a gift from Russia and are used only for special services. The original wooden bell, older than the metal bells, is used daily.

The **Library**, which houses some of the monastery's most extraordinary treasures, is closed to the general public. It has an almost unrivalled collection of precious Greek, Arabic, Syriac, Georgian, Armenian Coptic, Ethiopian and Slavonic manuscripts, reputedly second only to that of the Vatican. There are over 6000 books and over 3000 manuscripts, mostly in Greek, including the famous Codex Syriacus, a fifth-century translation of the gospels.

The monastery's small, but excellent, refurbished **museum** ① *E£25, students E£20, visit after 1000 when the initial crush has died down,* contains a collection of the gifts presented to the monastery over the centuries. The treasures were randomly scattered throughout the monastery until their accumulated worth was calculated by Friar Pachomius who then carefully gathered and preserved them in one place. Many interesting items have been lost over the ages, but it is fascinating to trace the routes of the pilgrims and of monks who sought alms through these treasures from cities as far-flung as Moscow and Calcutta. Also on display are a few of the monastery's 2000 priceless icons, a uniquely complete series with examples from every period, and a small selection of illuminated manuscripts from the library.

Because the monastery's **cemetery** in the gardens was so small, a custom developed of storing the overflow of monks' skeletons in the crypt of the Chapel of St Tryphon. This serves as the ossuary of the **Charnel House** that was in the monastery gardens. When a monk died his body was buried in the cemetery in the place of the oldest body, which was then removed to the Charnel House. The remains of the archbishops are kept separate in special niches. There's usually a queue to view this rather macabre room full of skeletons and skulls.

The monastery gardens are small. All the soil was carried here by the monks, who also constructed the water tanks for irrigation. It contains olive and apricot trees, plums and cherries with vegetables growing between. Immediately to the right of the monastery's main entrance at **Kleber's Tower**, which is about 15 m high and 3 m thick, is **Moses' Well**, which it is claimed has never dried up. It is supposed to be where the 40-year-old Moses, fleeing from Egypt, met one of Jethro's seven daughters whom he subsequently married.

Mount Sinai

If you've journeyed this far, attempt a climb up Mount Sinai (Jebel Musa), 2285 m, where, according to Muslim, Jewish and Christian tradition, Moses received the tablets of Law known as the Ten Commandments. The view is particularly spectacular at sunset and sunrise, when the mountain ranges are lit pink and gold. However, the vast majority make the traipse up for sunrise, setting off at an ungodly hour in the cold and dark to find it all but impossible to secure a good spot amidst the mass of blanket-wrapped forms at the summit. Those with limited time do this so as combine it with a visit the monastery (which is only open in the mornings). However, if you have a couple of days, it is better to start the ascent at about 1600 (an hour earlier in winter) in order to arrive at sunset. And, if you walk up via the more challenging steps, frequent solitary interludes can indeed feel spiritual and the passionate pilgrims met on the way only serve to intensify the experience. The 3700 steps, accessed from immediately behind the Monastery, are the shortest route (1½ to two hours), tough going and very difficult in the dark. Take a torch. The steps take you past the sixth-century **Elijah's Gate** and the **Shrive Gate** where pilgrims used to confess their sins to a priest before continuing their hike. You are supposed to take a guide with you, which police try to enforce, which is E£85 (you can negotiate this down). The path is less crowded and dirty than the other route, which is easier but indirect (about 2½ hours) and can be done on camel – there are plenty for hire behind the monastery for about E£100. Either way, the last 700 steps have to be done on foot and take another 30 minutes. Although there are refreshment stalls on the way up, getting more expensive nearer the summit, it is advisable to take at least two litres of water per person if making the ascent during the day. The stiff walk is quite rough and stout shoes and warm clothing are essential. On Mount Sinai is a chapel where services are performed on some Sundays by the monks and a mosque where a sheep is sacrificed

Blazing bushes and Catherine wheels

Mount Sinai marked the halfway point of the flight of the Jews from Egypt to the 'promised land'. Moses was clearly an inspirational leader for the incident of the burning bush led him to return to Egypt to lead his people to the land of milk and honey. But despite calling down from God the 10 plagues (frogs, lice, locusts, hail and fire among them), he failed to persuade the Pharaoh to release them from their slave labour. Finally the 80-year-old Moses asked God to strike the Egyptians with the passover when the Jews marked their houses with lamb's blood and were spared the massacre of all first-born children. As a result, the Pharoah banished the 600,000 Israelite men, women and children from Egypt. Their epic journey is related in the Book of Exodus in the Bible. They were pursued by the Egyptians (drowned after the Red Sea divided to allow the Israelites across), faced starvation (rescued with manna from heaven) and thirst (saved when a spring flowed from a rock Moses had struck with his staff) and defeated an attack by the Amaleks.

On Mount Sinai, Moses received the wisdom of the Ten Commandments, which have formed the code of practice for human behaviour for centuries.

The supposed site of the burning bush was developed into a monastery and in the 10th century named after Saint Catherine. According to legend Saint Catherine, who was born in AD 294 and was from a noble family in Alexandria, was a Christian convert who was martyred in the early fourth century for refusing to renounce her faith. She converted hundreds of people to Christianity and accused Emperor Maxentius of idolatry. When he tried to have her broken it was claimed that she shattered the spiked (Catherine) wheel by touching it, so Maxentius resorted to having her beheaded in Alexandria. After her execution her body vanished and according to legend was transported by angels to the top of Egypt's highest mountain, now named after her. Three centuries later this body was 'discovered', brought down from the mountain and placed in a golden casket in the church where it remains to this day.

once a year. Sleeping near the top is possible (see Where to stay, page 79) and blankets and mattresses are available for hire (E£10) around the summit.

Mount Catherine

At 2642 m Mount Catherine, or **Jebel Katrinah**, is Egypt's highest peak. It is about 6 km south of Mount Sinai and a five- to six-hour exhausting, but rewarding, climb. It is supposedly compulsory to take a guide, although it is possible to avoid detection and hike alone. Again, there are two routes up, one via the settlement of Arbayin (where you can see hyrax) that is longer but easier, and an steeper alternative route that has the appeal of being more natural. En route you pass the deserted **Monastery of the Forty Martyrs**. The path up to the summit was constructed by the monks who laid the granite staircase up Mount Sinai. On the summit there is a small chapel dedicated to St Catherine with water, a two-room hut for overnight pilgrims or trekkers, and a meteorological station.

Surrounding sights

About 50 km west of St Catherine lies **Wadi Feiran** ① *accessible by taxi from St Catherine for E£120, or get off the Cairo bus (from El Tor or from St Catherine's)*, a fertile winding valley filled with palms and wells. Some say this is where Moses left his people when he went to collect the Ten Commandments. Hence, a **monastery** dedicated to Moses lies at the valley's centre ① *T069-385 0071/2, open Mon-Sat 0900-1200, entrance free; if you wish to visit in the afternoon, pay a E£100 fee. Overnight guests welcome, see page 79*, where five Greek Orthodox nuns live and work. Visitors are admitted to view the two churches within the compound, decorated with icons and an iconostasis carved in Greece. The ruins of the original fourth century monastery are found adjacent to the complex, on a raised mound by the road. A kilometre or so further on from the monastery, in the direction of St Catherine's, are the lush wadi gardens where there are a couple of camps in which travellers can stay. There are several good and challenging hikes nearby. These, and longer treks, can be arranged with local guides on arrival. Wadi Feiran is a good destination for independent travellers, who wish to be flexible and don't want to be bound by any schedule. A reasonable amount to pay a guide is E£80 per day – not including food – and E£80 per camel, then another E£80 to cover administration costs and fees. A couple of kilometres along the road beyond the gardens is the Bedouin village of Wadi Feiran, though there is not much here to detain travellers save a couple of shops.

◉ The interior listings

For sleeping and eating price codes and other relevant information, see pages 11-15.

▣ Where to stay

St Catherine *p73*

Apart from the Monastery Guesthouse, most hotels and camps lie 2-3 km away from the monastery in the village of St Catherine, along 2 parallel main roads. Taxis between the village and monastery cost E£10.

€€€ St Catherine Village, Wadi El-Raha ('Valley of Repose'), T/F069-3470324-6, www.misrsinatitours.com. Every room has a view of the monastery in the distance up the valley. Twin-bed chalets of local stone, supposedly in the shape of a Bedouin tent, have been tastefully done out each with a lovely reception area and terrace. Often full in high season. 2 larger villas are available for US$110 per night.

€€ Daniela, T069-347 0379, www.daniela-hotels.com. Fairly spacious comfortable stone chalets, some with TV, all with heaters, are an easy walk from the village. The restaurant is reliable and tasty, serves Stella for E£15, and provides a good packed lunch for climbing mountains.

€€ El Wadi El-Mouquduss, T069-347 0225. Next to the **Daniela**, it's uninspiring from the outside but not bad value at E£250 half board or E£180 B&B for a double. Nice bathrooms, good heaters, some rooms have balconies (which look down on a murky pool), most have TV (or enquire about their cheaper more basic rooms). The buffets are good, with 10 types of salad as well as the usual meat/rice /veg combo (lunch E£30, dinner E£40).

€€ Monastery Guesthouse, T069-347 0353. It's not cheap, but spend a night here if you can afford it. Being able to wander around the outer walls whenever the mood takes you (and in relative isolation) is the best way to appreciate the monastery. Plus the orchards and gardens are beautiful and restful, the rooms attractive and warm. Cost includes half board, triple and quadruple rooms are also available. It's wise to reserve ahead, especially during the common pilgrimage months of Apr and Aug. If you want to go for lunch or dinner, give 24 hrs' advance warning, and if you can't actually stay here then a drink in the courtyard coffee shop is next best thing (alcohol is served), open 0700 until late (except on Fri/Sat nights, when it closes at 2100 to reopen 2400-0300).

€ Bedouin Camp, Al-Milga, T069-347 0457, T010-641 3575, www.sheikhmousa.com, near the bus stop, uphill past the square and petrol station. Basic but clean concrete rooms have blankets and screen doors (essential in summer). Dorm beds available, all share a bathroom with hot water and there's space to put up tents. The washing machine is a real bonus. This is the place to come to organize a trekking excursion to the high mountains.

€ El-Karm Ecolodge, Wadi Gharbah, T069-347 0032/3, www.ecolodges.sahara safaris.org/alkarm. Manager Jameel Ataya can be contacted on his mobile, T010-132 4693, but only speaks Arabic (though if you leave a message in English someone will get back to you). Alternatively, contact **Bedouin Camp** in St Catherine's for help with reservations, T069-347 0457. Deep in the heart of the south Sinai mountains, accessible by 4WD from El Tarfa village, a lift from St Catherine's is E£130-150 or if you get off the bus at El Tarfa (west of St Catherine's), Jameel can arrange a pick-up from there for the last 30 mins along a bumpy track, E£50. The eco-lodge is fully managed and operated by the Jabaliya tribe with the aim of preserving the traditions of Bedouin culture. Old ruins have been rebuilt to create 8 simple stone rooms that sleep 3-7 people. The setting and isolation are splendid, the walking superb, and a visit here is a special experience. Room only is E£50 per person, E£120 full board. Camping is E£30, use of the kitchen E£10. Though there are blankets, it's a good idea to bring your own sleeping bag (certainly in winter). You can arrange half- or full-day treks from here, or visit the Nabatean ruins nearby, or the dry waterfall at Seida Nughra is a 2-hr

walk away. El-Karm feels like the ultimate getaway: it is rare to be somewhere so isolated and untouristed and yet still have a bed to retire to and delicious food.

€ Farag Fox Desert Camp, between the monastery and town centre, T069-347 0344, T010-698 7807. A good choice and the cheapest in town. Nestling by an olive orchard, clean, attractive huts with plenty of blankets are E£30 per person and decent shared baths have hot water (E£40 with private bath). You can camp down here for E£10 per tent, or there are a couple of alluring stone-walled gardens 10-20 mins' walk up the valley, with fresh water supply, where you can meditate in complete isolation under the stars (they can provide tents/blankets). Otherwise evenings are spent lolling around in the Bedouin tent drinking free tea around the fire, while candles twinkle on the rocks surrounding the camp. It's run by 2 local Bedouin brothers who also organize trips through the desert plateaus (as opposed to trekking in the high mountains), costing around E£175-200 per person depending upon the size of the group.

Camping

Apart from the great camping spots at Fox Camp (above), most visitors spend the night on Mt Sinai to see the sunrise. The altitude makes for sub-zero night-time temperatures for much of the year – a torch, good sleeping bag and warm clothing are absolutely essential. It is possible to rent blankets and mattresses around the summit for E£10.

Wadi Feiran *p78*

€€€-€€ Holy Monastery of the Prophet Moses, T069-385 0071/2, sinai.oasisfaran@yahoo.gr. Hidden within the walled compound of a monastery, guest-rooms are spotless and comfortable. The price includes a good breakfast and dinner, and there are some cheaper rooms which share bathrooms. Palms, frangipani and the historic churches all make for a special stay.

€ Greenland , T018-463 2465. Located in the Feiran gardens and identified by a sign next to the road offering tea, the 'Garden of Flowers' has sleeping space under a Bedouin shade on rag-rugs surrounded by blossoming bougainvillea, herb gardens and date palms. There is electricity. Adjacent are 2 other camps (**Beit Al-Shar** and **Holy Oasis**) offering similarly basic accommodation.

Restaurants

St Catherine p73

The hotels and camps all provide a similar buffet lunch (E£25-30) and dinner (E£30-50) of rice, macaroni, meat, chicken and veg, plus soup at dinner time. There are a couple of restaurants in the village serving the standard fare but for around E£15, but they sometimes close as early as 1900. The **Monastery Guesthouse** also provides decent meals at a reasonable cost of E£25, though they need a day's warning. For a change, there is an OK *koshary* place to the left of the post office. For *tamaya*, go to the stall next to the bank.

Shopping

St Catherine p73

Fansina, T069-347 0155, past **Fox Camp** on the left on the way into the village. Sat-Thu 1000-1500. Local Bedouin businesswoman Selima works with over 450 women from tribes all over South Sinai to produce gifts and textiles, including *galabiyas* and intricate beadwork trinkets, all at fixed prices. Articles incorporate ancestral designs that would have adorned practical items (such as the bags girls took out when herding goats, or pouches made for nomadic husbands to carry their sugar and tea). Her new premises opened early 2008, the cool interior and shady outdoor area are inviting, Selima herself is quite an inspiration.

There are a couple of gifts shops at the monastery, the better one is in front of the guesthouse. In the village, provisions can be bought at **Supermarket Katreen**, plus a couple of other small grocery stores, bakery, bazaar and petrol station.

What to do

St Catherine p73

Trekking

Besides the well-trampled peaks of Mt Sinai and, to a lesser extent, Mt St Catherine, trekking opportunities in Central and South Sinai abound. Information about day treks are available at the **St Catherine's National Park Visitor Centre** and online at www.touregypt.net/walkingtours. To explore in depth any of the surrounding peaks you must have a Bedouin guide. Trekking alone is impossible (as well as dangerous). The perfect month, temperature-wise, is May. Jul and Aug are unbearably hot all day, and you have to be pretty hardy to consider a winter trek.

Safaris that visit the desert areas, wadis and lower peaks are generally arranged in Nuweiba or Dahab, or through **Farag Fox Safaris** in St Catherine's, T069-347 0344, using guides from the tribes that inhabit these areas. If you are embarking on a long safari that visits more than one territory, you will transfer between camels and guides to those of another tribe (but retain a head guide from the original party) so that you are always in the hands of those who know the region best. If you are satisfied with your guide and the experience, you may wish to tip (E£80-100 is an acceptable amount).

Some highlights of the area include: **Galt El-Azraq**, a striking and beautiful 7-m-deep spring-fed crystal-clear pool nestled in the rock, an arduous 1-day walk so most people chose to do it as a 2-day trek from St Catherine's. **Wadi Shaqq** is a large canyon beyond Jebel Katrinah, with beautiful *bustans* (orchards) and a hermit's cell and monastery. There are some Bedouin buildings here (some still inhabited) and others that are set up for trekkers with compost toilets, a shower and rock-cut rooms. **Jebel Umm Shomar** is the second tallest peak in Egypt, from where there are staggering views as far as the coastal sandy plains of **El-Tur**. Hikes to/from here visit tiny Bedouin settlements, lush wadis with immense boulders among the date palms, and Byzantine ruins. It's possible to walk from St Catherine's to El-Tur in 3-5 days, via Umm Shomar. **Wadi Nugra** is a rocky valley with a rain-fed 20-m-high waterfall that trickles off mossy boulders into pools perfect for cooling off, in between Nuweiba and St Catherine's, a 3-day trek from St Catherine's. **Sheikh Awad's Tomb** is a picturesque oasis containing the holy man's shrine, a well and a small Bedouin community, a 3-day trek from St Catherine's. Another destination is the unfinished palace of **Abbas Pasha** at 4-hr climb to a summit that affords some of the best views of the high mountains and distant lowlands; a circular trek starting from St Catherine's takes 5 days. **The Blue Valley** is a bizarre sprawl of desert 12 km from St Catherine interspersed with boulders painted blue in the late 1970s by a Belgian artist. Claims as to why he did it vary; there's a common saying in Arabic, "There will be peace with Israel when the sky meets the desert", an impossibility, of course. So the artist, in an attempt to make real the impossible, met with both Prime Minister Rabin and President Sadat to offer his idea in the name of peace, and painted the rock blue to bring the sky to the desert. A noble tale ... ask your guide for his version of the story.

Most treks tend to be circular, starting and finishing at the same point, although an A–B route is possible (from St Catherine's to El-Tur, for example). Also, many of the areas mentioned above can be linked together to form longer hikes of 15 days or more. **Mountain Tours**, T069-347 0457, headed up by Sheikh Mousa, is good for those who don't like to plan too much in advance. Sheikh Mousa will take your passport, and secure the necessary permit, guide, camels, food

and equipment. Tell him how much time you have and what you want to see and he'll help create an itinerary. Cost is €30 per person per day, everything included, for a group of at least 3 (more than E50 for 1 person). You may wish to bring water-purification tablets if drinking spring water is a concern. **Sheikh Sina Bedouin Treks**, T069-347 0880, www.sheikhsina.com, are good for multiple-day treks. They work alongside Sheikh Mousa and the local community to further the empowerment of the Bedouin tribes. A rotating system of guides and cameleers ensures that each family has a turn benefiting from the tours and an emphasis is placed on sustainable tourism. Guides speak English, French and German and have been trained in first-aid, which could be vital up here.

⊖ Transport

St Catherine p73

Bus There are direct buses for the 8-hr journey between St Catherine and **Cairo** at 0600 and occasionally at 1300 (E£60) via **Suez**, and supposedly one to **Dahab** (1300, E£25) though more often than not, this doesn't run. Check at the bus station for the latest schedules.

Taxis
Service taxis If a microbus has come from **Dahab** the night before, it will return from St Catherine at 1100, departing from next to the mosque (E£40 1-way or E£50 return). Micros leave when full between 0600-1300 for **Suez**, E£20-30, or E£350 to hire the whole vehicle. Travellers can share the cost of hiring a 7-seat service taxi to **Dahab** (E£200-250 per car), **Sharm El-Sheikh** (E£300-450), **Nuweiba** (E£200), or other towns in the peninsula.

❶ Directory

St Catherine p73
Medical services Next to the tourist police opposite the bus station, not recommended, make the journey to Sharm if you can.

Northern Sinai

The vast majority of tourists coming to Sinai only visit the Gulf of Aqaba coastline and St Catherine's Monastery, and this is for good reason. Although the northern part of the peninsula has a number of attractions both in El-Arish and along the 210-km Mediterranean coastline stretching from Port Said to the border at Rafah, these are low-key in comparison to the temptations of the Red Sea and interior. Distinctly different in feel from the red rugged south, Northern Sinai has softer charms, with palm-fringed beaches and creamy sand dunes that melt into Mediterranean lagoons. Birdwatchers will find fulfilment in the Zaranik Protectorate Reserve, while El-Arish appeals to those who like to mix a taste of the beach with a gritty dash of Bedouin culture. As the situation on the Rafah border grows ever more tense, very few travellers make it this far – either as a destination or en route to Israel.

Arriving in Northern Sinai
Getting there The road east from Ismailia crosses the Suez Canal Bridge, also known as the Japanese–Egyptian Friendship Bridge, which rises bizarrely out of the desert and affords brief views down the length of the canal. Coming from Suez further south, the road goes through the Ahmed Hamdi Tunnel.

Pelusium and Lake Bardweel
The road to El-Arish passes through some wild-looking towns, next to huge dunes and goat-herders roaming among the scrub, and past small enclaves of nomadic settlements. About 40 km along the road from Qantara to El-Arish there is a signpost for **Pelusium** ⓘ *daily 0900-1600*. The road is surfaced until it crosses a small canal. Turn left on to the next (unsurfaced) road. This road is not passable after rain – be prepared to walk from the tarmac. If you have your own transport and official permission you can visit these Roman ruins, also known as Tel El-Farame. The site covers a wide area, littered with ancient rubble, stone, bricks and columns, of which the highlight is the partially uncovered amphitheatre. The city was situated on a now dry tributary of the Nile and guarded access from the east and acted as a customs post. It is mentioned in the Bible as 'the stronghold of Egypt'. The Persians came through here and both Pompey and Baldwin I ended their days here in tragic circumstances.

Lake Bardweel (66,500 ha) is important for fish such as mullet and seabass as well as migratory birds but access to the shore is often difficult. At the eastern end is the **Zaranik Protectorate** where over 200 species of migrating bird have been recorded. This area is of such significance that it has been preserved as a wetland under the auspices of UNESCO. Take the track north at the hamlet of Al-Sabeka (the sign says keep to the road but forgets to mention the landmines).

El-Arish → *For listings, see pages 85-86.*

This town, 180 km east of the Suez Canal, is the governorate capital of North Sinai and used to be noted for its 30 km of palm-lined fine white-sand beach. El-Arish means palm huts in Arabic, of which you won't see many these days as – like so many other places along the coast of Sinai – concrete has become the dominant feature. Still, it's a quiet, bumbling sort of place, good for family getaways or groups of friends who may wish to rent somewhere on the beach and enjoy one another's company and not much else. The Bedouins of Northern Sinai weave beautiful fabrics and rugs, which are brightly displayed at the sprawling weekly *souk*. The new museum is a tragically empty edifice, beautifully laid out and lit, with exquisite pharaonic, Islamic, Coptic and Bedouin displays. Al-Nakheel to the east is the best beach at El-Arish with famous but depleted palm trees extending the length of the shoreline. Also very noticeable in El-Arish is the high proportion of limbless beggars, victims of landmines.

Arriving in El-Arish

Getting around The town consists of two main streets, Sharia Fouad Abu Zakry, which runs along the beach, and Sharia 23rd July, which runs perpendicular to the beach and finishes up at Midan Baladiya. The bus and long-distance service taxi stations are 2 km west of the town centre, a E£5 ride from most hotels. From Midan Baladiya it is a 2- to 3-km walk or minibus ride (50 pt) to Fouad Abu Zakry and the beach.

Information There is an almost useless Egyptian General Authority for the Promotion of Tourism office ① *T068-336 3743, Sat-Thu 0900-1400*, in the same office as the Tourist Police ① *T068-335 9490*, on Sharia Fouad Abu Zakry. The main police station is on Sharia El-Geish on the way to Rafah.

Places in El-Arish

The El-Arish Museum ① *on the Rafah road, T068-3324 105, Sat-Thu 0900-1330, E£5 in a taxi or 50 pt by micro, tickets E£20, students E£10, cameras E£20, it might be worth paying to take a camera in, as the lighting throws up dramatic shadows and reliefs on the pharaonic exhibits*. This huge temple-like edifice, built to cope with stampedes of visitors of which there are virtually none, is overstaffed to a spectacular degree even by Egyptian standards. Opened in April 2008, it is an almost perfect museum experience except for the fact that the labelling fails to inform you where any of the items originate from – but if you have made it as far as El-Arish, this is not to be missed. The first couple of rooms display majestic pharaonic pieces, with helpful diagrammatic murals to illustrate how the reliefs fitted into temple friezes; worthy of note are the displays dedicated to Hathor in her various guises, sometimes represented as a cow and other times as a human with a cow's ears. The Islamic collection incorporates an intricate *mashrabiya* window with stained-glass panels and immense draperies from the *Ka'ba*, as from 1223-1962 a factory in Cairo was the main manufacturer of the embroidered cloth that covers the holiest place of Islam. As well as an array of Coptic icons, there is a small coin room where accompanying text actually manages to make the minting techniques and politics of ancient currencies interesting. Further on, in the basement, the heritage of Sinai is brought to life through a beautiful collection of chunky jewellery, vicious swords and daggers, adornments for camels, and the most heavily embroidered *gallabiyas* imaginable. Cumbersome *borga* veils, heavy with chains, tassels, hundreds of coins, seeds, beads and embroidery remind you what an extraordinary culture still inhabits this land.

The Thursday Bedouin market (*Souk El-Khamees*), in the oldest part of town, is best reached from Midan Baladiya, just follow the crowds. If you are in El-Arish on a Thursday, it's a good notion to visit the museum to see the Bedouin designs and handiwork before moving on to the weekly market to haggle over newly crafted versions of any designs that took your fancy. You'll need to get up early as mornings are most fun among the endless piles of aubergines, T-shirts, crockery and condiments all laid out on the ground. Prices for Bedouin trinkets are reasonable and the dress of the women who have journeyed here to sell goods is not a million miles away from that on display in the museum. **El-Arish Fortress** is on a plateau to the southwest of the town on the remains of an ancient pharaonic castle. Beside the pieces of aqueduct, and hidden behind wooden walls (absolutely no entry) where excavations are taking place, are the ruins of the fort rebuilt by the Turk Sultan Sulayman Al Qanouni in 1560 and demolished in the First World War by British bombardment. There is a small zoo, east of town opposite the museum, but it's not worth the visit. Between Abi-Sakl to the west and the zoo to the east is the harbour, used mainly by fishing vessels (fishing permits may be granted). The village of Kilometre 21 hosts a camel-racing festival in August/September each year, which attracts competitors from Libya and the Gulf countries. Otherwise pastimes in El-Arish tend to revolve around the beach.

The **Zaranik Protectorate** ⓘ *around 30 km east of town, US$5 per person and US$5 per car*, encompasses the eastern shore of Lake Bardaweel and extends north to the sea. It is a wildlife haven protected since the mid-1980s. In September, thousands of birds (up to 270 different species, including flamingo) stop here en route from Europe to Africa. It's also an important turtle site. At the entrance of the protectorate, there is an informative visitor centre that shows films. It costs E£25-30 to get here in a taxi from El-Arish (it is not possible to get off the bus by the turn-off to the park and walk, it's too far from the main highway). There are several campsites for US$10 per person per night and there are 10 (new) double rooms available. It's best to bring your own food and use their kitchen, and there's a washing machine, fridge, binoculars and telescopes for guests' use. To arrange a visit – one day's notice is requested – call Mr Saat (director of the protectorate) on T010-544 2641.

Border crossing to Palestine and Israel
It is no longer possible to cross to Israel/Gaza at the Rafah and all travellers now use the Taba border crossing.

◉ Northern Sinai listings

For sleeping and eating price codes and other relevant information, see pages 11-15.

● Where to stay

El-Arish *p82*

During the Jul-Sep high season it may be difficult to find a room on the beach without pre-booking. During the winter most hotels are quiet and some shut down, but the ones listed below are open whatever the season. In the town centre there are a few acceptable budget options, should you just need to crash for a night.

€€€€ Swiss Inn Resort, Sharia Fouad Abu Zakry, T068-335 1321. Previously the **Oberoi**, some of the brass, marble and wood remains in public areas, while rooms have huge beds and sea views. Recreation facilities include health spa, tennis courts, a large saltwater pool and another (more attractive) freshwater one. There's a well-stocked bar and beer is also available at the coffee shop, where outside guests congregate. High season is US$180 half board, otherwise it's a bargain at E£25 to use the pool and lovely private beach for the day.

€ Greenland Beach, Sharia Fouad Abu Zakry, T068-336 0601. Recently repainted in lurid yellows with peach tiled floors, some rooms have views of the sea (and of rooftops) and the bathrooms are decent. However, single female travellers would do best to avoid staying here. No breakfast.

€ Macca Hotel (no English sign) on Sharia Al-Salam, a side street off the northern end of Sharia 23 July, T068-335 2632, F068-335 2632. Mercifully free from traffic noise, the **Macca** is bustly and bright and staff are friendly and effective. All in all, it is a good choice and rooms have balconies and baths. The restaurant is cheap and decent, breakfast is included, doubles E£105 singles E£75.

€ Moon Light, Sharia Fouad Abu Zakry. A funny faded peeling kind of a place, with chalet rooms around a scruffy garden. The beach is a few steps away but is rather littered, yet it is often busy, has the potential to be fun if you're in a group, and is cheap. The cafeteria has drinks but no food.

€ Safa Hotel, Sharia 23 July, T068-335 3798. Best of the bottom-rung choices in town with a variety of rooms in different configurations spread over several floors. Freshly painted and most rooms are bright – although they don't have the cleanest linens or bathrooms in the world. On arrival, you can ask for clean sheets and towels, and the staff try their best. No breakfast.

Camping

Camping is permitted in the Zaranik Protectorate, US$5 a night. It may be possible to camp on the beach if you can get permission from the police.

❼ Restaurants

El-Arish *p82*

Besides the hotels and a series of stalls by the beach that sell *fuul* and other standards, there are a few cheap restaurants and *ahwas* (with *sheesha*) in and around Midan Baladiya.

€€ Basata, in the western part of town. Offers a pleasant atmosphere with good seafood, geared more towards tourists.

€ Batebat, diagonally opposite Aziz, focuses on meat. Good *tagens*, *koftas* and chicken.

€ Sammar and **Aziz** on Sharia Tahrir just north of Midan Baladiya, serve up good cheap grilled food with a variety of salads.

€ Tahrir Fuul stand, near Aziz, no English sign just ask around, churns out excellent *fuul* sandwiches. Or try the narrow *souk* street, just north of Aziz restaurant, where there is another local joint on the left that has an excellent array of salads and sandwich fillings and a small seating area inside.

🎭 Entertainment

El-Arish *p82*

Nightlife in El-Arish thrives around the cafés of Midan Baladiya, where no matter the night, you will find people puffing on *sheesha* pipes, sipping tea and playing backgammon. El-Arish is a rather conservative community and there aren't many places that serve alcohol. The safest bet is the **Swiss Inn**, which has a well-stocked bar and a pleasant outside coffee shop that serves beer.

🛍 Shopping

El Arish *p82*

There are some rather sleazy tourist shops on Sharia 23 July but for quality items it is better to bargain at the Bedouin market.

🚌 Transport

El Arish *p82*

Bus
East Delta Bus Co, T068-332 5931 run several daily buses between El-Arish and **Cairo** (4-5 hrs, E£26-32), and 1 per day to **Ismailia** and **Qantara**, where you have to change for **Port Said**. The bus terminal is a couple of kilometres east of Midan Baladiya, accessible by microbus.

Taxis
Service taxis to/from **Midan Koulali Terminal** in **Cairo** (5 hrs, E£30): **Midan El-Gomhoriyya** in **Ismailia** (3 hrs, E£15) or by the Suez Canal in **Qantara** (2½ hrs, E£12). To get to **Port Said** there is a free ferry across the canal from East to West Qantara, from where you can either board another service or a train. Taxis to **Cairo** leave early morning.

Minibuses run back and forth from the *souk* to the beach and around town (50 pt), as do 1970s 'stretch' Mercedes.

🏛 Directory

El Arish *p82*
Medical services Mubarak International Hospital, T068-332 4018/9, should be your 1st choice, otherwise **El-Arish General Hospital**, Sharia El-Geish, T068-336 1077.

Contents

Footprint features

Red Sea & Eastern Desert

At a glance

◔ **Getting around** Buses and service taxis between the main towns, then taxis to the resorts. There are flights to Marsa Alam. Catamarans cross the Gulf of Suez from Hurghada to Sharm El-Sheikh.

◔ **Time required** At least a week if you're planning on both diving and desert exploration.

◔ **Weather** Searingly hot between May and mid-Sep.

✕ **When not to go** If you want to do an extended desert excursion, avoid summer as tours do not run during this time.

South of Suez

The Red Sea coast stretches down from Suez towards Hurghada, encompassing the resorts and enclaves around Ain Soukna and becoming progressively more beautiful and unspoilt as it extends further south. Inland from Zafarana, the Red Sea monasteries are Egypt's oldest and attract thousands of Coptic pilgrims to the desert hinterland. The plush and extensive resorts of El-Gouna, built on a succession of islands, tempt wealthy Cairenes and Western package tourists with their good diving and high-class dining. El-Gouna often feels more like Europe than it does Egypt, and is easily connected to the capital by twice-weekly flights or a five-hour bus ride.

Aïn Sukhna → For listings, see pages 91-93.

Only two hours from Cairo, on the Red Sea about 60 km south of Suez, the shoreline of Aïn Sukhna is a popular getaway for middle class and wealthy Cairenes seeking respite from the chaos of the capital. Although it lacks the breadth of sea life that thrives further south, and the horizon is perpetually dotted with huge oil tankers, it still retains the beauty of a Red Sea shoreline and makes a convenient beach stop for anyone based in Cairo if time is limited. It's supposed to be a region of hot springs, hence its name (which does literally mean 'hot springs'), but the appeal centres much more around the sandy beaches and resort culture. The location of Sukhna also makes it a popular spot for birdwatchers, as it's on the raptor migration route. There are no budget hotels, just several resorts, most offering water sports, snorkelling, fishing and lots of restaurants, pools and other activities. If you want solitude, avoid Sukhna on the weekends.

Zafarana and the Red Sea monasteries

From Aïn Sukhna, an ugly swathe of construction stretches almost the entire distance to Zafarana, 62 km south on H44 at the junction to Beni Suef. The most noticeable feature to the north of the town is a wind farm with hundreds of towering turbines. For travellers, the small community of Zafarana is really just an access point to the two isolated monasteries of St Anthony's and St Paul's, and where there is an acceptable hotel that independent travellers can utilise if intending to visit both the monasteries. St Anthony's and St Paul's lie hidden in the folds of the Red Sea mountains, and are the oldest in Egypt. Pilgrim tours to these monasteries are organized by the **Coptic Patriarch** ① 22 Sharia Ramsis, Abbassiya, Cairo T02-2591 7360, and foreign tourists are welcome to join. No-one (save for young men who are considering the monastic life) is allowed to stay at St Anthony's, while St Paul's is less likely to leave you bed-less in the desert (although this may involve sleeping by the gatehouse).

Getting there
Day tours to the monasteries are offered by a number of Hurghada travel agents including **Misr Travel**, see page 104. Otherwise a group can negotiate a single price with a local taxi from Hurghada, Suez or Cairo. Provided it is not too hot and you take enough water it is also possible to get part way to St Anthony's by service taxi, from Beni Suef or

Zafarana. Service taxis leave from the road behind the NPCO petrol station. A blue and white sign 35 km from Zafarana indicates the monastery, from where there are still 15 km more to go on foot, unless you manage to hitch a lift. You could hire a vehicle from Zafarana to take you for about E£50. For St Pauls, the Hurghada to Cairo/Suez bus can drop you at the turn-off, approximately 24 km south of Zafarana, which is indicated with blue and white signs. From here, the road leads about 12 km up a slight incline but, again, you may well be able to hitch a ride. Be aware that trying to visit either of the monasteries in one day by public transport/hitching and walking is a tall order, and it would be foolish to attempt both unless you are intending to stay in Zafarana at the end of the day. It's a tough 30-km trek over a plateau between the two monasteries, and this should never be embarked upon without a guide. This can be arranged in Zafarana with local Bedouin; try asking the manager of the Sahara Inn to assist you. Note that St Paul's only opens on Fridays, Saturdays and Sundays during the fasting period from 25 November to 7 January, and that St Anthony's only opens on Fridays, Saturdays and Sundays during the fasting time of Lent (55 days) from about mid-February to mid-April, depending on the Coptic calendar.

St Anthony's Monastery

ⓘ *Daily 0400-1645 except during Lent (Feb to mid-Apr) when it only opens Fri, Sat and Sun. A monk who is fluent in your language will be assigned to give a tour.*

Known locally as Deir Amba Antonyus this is the more important of the two monasteries for Coptic pilgrims, and attracts more foreign visitors than St Paul's to admire its extraordinary and bright wall paintings. The Christian monastic tradition has its origin in the community that established itself here in the fourth century, and the daily rituals still observed have hardly changed in the last 16 centuries.

The 'father of monasticism' St Anthony (AD 251-356) was born in the small village of **Koma Al-Arus**. He became a hermit after he was orphaned at 18 just before the height of the persecution against the Christians by Emperor Diocletian (AD 284-305). By AD 313 not only was Christianity tolerated but it had also been corrupted by its adoption as the state religion. This led to increasing numbers of hermits following Anthony's example and seeking isolation in desert retreats (see St Catherine's monastery, page 73). After his death, at the reported age of 105, the location of his grave was kept secret but a small chapel was erected that became the foundation of the monastery.

In the course of its history it has been subject to attacks from the Bedouin tribes in the eighth and ninth centuries and the Nasir Al-Dawla who destroyed it in the 11th century. It was restored in the 12th century by monks from throughout the Coptic world, only to be badly damaged again in the 15th century when the monks were massacred by rebellious servants. Syrian monks were sent to rebuild it in the mid-16th century and it was subsequently inhabited by a mixture of Coptic, Ethiopian and Syrian monks. Its importance rose and many 17th- to 19th-century Coptic patriarchs were chosen from among its monks; by the 18th century it was receiving increasing numbers of European visitors. The result is that the five-church monastery has developed into an enormous complex containing all the commodities of a village. There is a free canteen and a couple of souvenir shops. The outer walls, some sections of which can be walked along, span 2 km. Around 120 monks now reside within the complex.

St Anthony's Church, parts of which date back to the 13th century, is the oldest church in the complex. Relatively recent cleaning and restoration has revealed the fabulous colours of paintings covering each and every wall, previously preserved under centuries of soot and grime. While inside, try to identify the apostles in the picture on the south wall. The faces of the camels, horses and martyrs which are depicted are strikingly natural. Tradition always held that the relics of St Anthony lay beneath the altar, and a recent survey has confirmed that there is indeed a tomb below. There are four other churches in the complex. **St Mark's Church** dates from 1766 and is reputed to contain the relics of St Mark the Evangelist in a chest on the north wall, though this is normally closed to foreign visitors. You will also be shown the ancient **refectory**, containing a sixth-century stone table and the spring that St Anthony discovered which still provides all the monastery's water needs today.

The **Cave of St Anthony**, 276 m above and 2 km northeast of the monastery, is a steep walk but the view alone from the terrace in front of the cave, 690 m above the Red Sea, justifies the climb. From the monastery, a 15-minute walk along a gravel road leads to the modern Church of the Christ and the Resurrection, from where steps lead up for a painful 30- to 45-minute climb to the cave. The cave, where St Anthony is supposed to have spent the last 25 years of his life, consists of a tunnel (which is a tight squeeze) leading to a dark chamber. The decorations on the walls are medieval graffiti often complemented by more recent additions in the shape of supplications stuck into the cracks of the walls by visiting pilgrims. Take water, a hat and a torch with you for this mini-expedition, and be warned it is quite a tough walk with no shade. Shoes should be left outside the entrance to the cave.

St Paul's Monastery

① *Daily 0530-1700 except during Lent and between 25 Nov and 7 Jan, when the monastery only opens on Fri, Sat and Sun.*

The smaller Monastery of St Paul was built around the cave where St Paul the Theban (AD 228-348) spent his life. Although the dates do not actually match, he is supposed to have fled the persecution of **Decius** (AD 249-251) and arrived in the eastern desert from Alexandria at the age of 16. He is the earliest hermit on record and was visited by St Anthony to whom he gave a tunic of palm leaves. St Paul apparently acknowledged him as his spiritual superior and St Anthony's Monastery has always overshadowed that of St Paul both theologically and architecturally. It is now home to a community of around 90 monks.

The larger of the two churches is dedicated to St Michael and there are two sanctuaries. The south one is dedicated to St John the Baptist where a strange 18th-century gilded icon depicts the saint's head on a dish. The **Church of St Paul** contains the actual cave where he lived and what are claimed to be his relics, which were preserved during the many raids on the monastery. The worst of these was in 1484, when Bedouin tribes massacred the entire population of monks and occupied the monastery for the following 80 years. Things are rather more tranquil now, though the tour buses of Coptic pilgrims can cause a bit of a stir.

El-Gouna → *For listings, see pages 91-93.*

The upmarket resort of El-Gouna is just 25 km (30 minutes in a taxi) north of Hurghada but a million miles away in terms of ambiance and aesthetics. It attracts a far more sedate foreign crowd, mainly families and couples, plus wealthy Egyptians who come to their private villas on weekends and public holidays. All the hotel developments and villas have been constructed in a Nubian/Arabesque style and are dotted across a series of beautiful islands interlinked by seawater lagoons. There are also many uninhabited islands and coral reefs that are exposed only at low tide. With its collection of chic restaurants and cosy inns overlooking a harbour brimming with colourful sails, a stroll down the boardwalk is a delight. Shuttle buses run from the hotels to the heart of El-Gouna, where an immaculate square is surrounded by tasteful shops and sophisticated restaurants and the pedestrianized cobbled streets are lit by pottery lanterns. It doesn't look or feel like anywhere else in Egypt, and for many travellers the effect is too plastic and surreal to warrant an extended stay (there are no budget hotels in town anyway), but for a special evening out away from the tacky bustle of Hurghada, El-Gouna certainly delivers quality and class. The **information office** ① *open 0900-2300*, can provide good maps and information about the area, or check www.elgouna.com. Useful telephone numbers: **emergency** ① *T065-358 0011*; **hyperbaric chamber** ① *T012-218 7550.* ▸▸ *For diving information for the Red Sea, see pages 53 and 54.*

◉ South of Suez listings

For sleeping and eating price codes and other relevant information, see pages 11-15.

🛏 Where to stay

Zafarana *p88*

€ Sahara Inn, T012-2363 445/6. This decent if simple hotel has 4 large rooms in the new wing sharing a spacious terrace, with TV, a/c and hot water in the clean white rooms. There are also 8 rooms in the older wing with fans, bathrooms and TV but no balcony. The kind manager will negotiate on price. Breakfast is not included. The restaurant is tourist-friendly.

El-Gouna *p91*

Almost all hotels in El-Gouna are top-class and rather beautiful, both design and location-wise. Although they are totally self-contained with all the facilities you could desire, unlike some of the big resorts along this coast the nightlife of the town is easily accessible and you are not confined to your hotel for an evening's entertainment. Any accommodation in El-Gouna can be booked online at www.elgouna.com.

€€€€ Movenpick, 30 km from airport, T065-354 4501, www.moevenpick-hotels. com. Built from terracotta, in gardens with tropical plants and palms framed by the desert behind and the lagoon in front. There are 4 pools, health club, a selection of bars and restaurants including **El-Sayadin** on the beach and a great Thai restaurant, and children's club. **Angsana Spa** is one of Egypt's most luxurious.

€€€ Captain's Inn, T065-358 0170. Cosy and comfy rooms overlooking Abu Tig Marina, free shuttle buses run to the lagoon. Use of the next door hotel's pool.

€€€ Dawar El-Omda, central El-Gouna, T065-358 0063-6, www.dawarelomda-elgouna.com. A smaller hotel, with comfortable rooms furnished in traditional Egyptian style although they are slightly showing their age. The hotel's name literally means 'Omda's home' (chief's home) and the design resembles an Egyptian community leader's house. The pool is delightful, frequent boats run to Zaytona beach and the outside restaurant/bar is the perfect place for an evening drink among soft lamplight and flowering trees. Some of the cheapest beds in El-Gouna, surprisingly.

🍴 Restaurants

Zafarana *p88*

€€ Sahara Inn. The cleanest and most tourist-orientated place to eat between Cairo and Hurghada, with pizza, fish and alcohol available.

€ Horus Cafeteria, near the police checkpoint on the road north to Cairo. Decent Egyptian meals and breakfast are available on the large terrace of this local haunt, and the toilets are acceptable. No English sign.

El-Gouna *p91*

Among the most upmarket of resorts in Egypt, dining well in El-Gouna takes little effort. Restaurants tend to congregate around each other, making menu perusing easy.

€€€ Biergarten, Kafr El-Gouna, varied menu from *wurst* and *sauerkraut* to spaghetti. Dancing on Wed.

€€€ Bleu Bleu, Abu Tig Marina, T065-549702-4. Unquestionably El-Gouna's most elegant restaurant, the French cuisine is superb and set in lovely environs.

€€€ El-Sayadin, Movenpick Hotel, T065-354 4501. Truly excellent fish in an amazing beachside setting, plus some Oriental delicacies.

€€€ Kiki's, Kafr El-Gouna. A wide selection of authentic Italian food (Italian-owned), there's intimate indoor seating or the outdoor terrace overlooking the lagoon.

€€€-€€ Club House, www.elgounaclub house.com, opposite Dawar El-Omda. Try the lunch selection of Italian-inspired food, freshly prepared. As the population of El-Gouna is largely Coptic, they have developed a good range of vegetarian dishes to fit in with the frequent fasting. It's also a friendly and bustling place for a drink by the pool.

€€ Tamr Henna, T065-358 0521. Mixture of Turkish, Egyptian and Italian dishes, there's something for everyone, it's also the best place to have a *sheesha* and people-watch in the main square. There's also an a/c interior.

🍸 Bars and nightclubs

El-Gouna *p91*
Besides the standard hotel bars, there are several funky places to go for a drink:
Barten, at the end of the marina. Intimate bar with modern decor highlighted by red lights and minimal furniture. Popular with young trendy Cairenes.

Mangroovy Beach Bar, special seafood dinners with dancing round the bonfire on Sun and Wed. Access by shuttle bus.

Sand Bar, Kafr El-Gouna. Small in size but with a lively atmosphere, cheap draught beer, good selection of wine and tasty bar snacks, cold beer and loud music, very popular with divers.

🏔 What to do

El-Gouna *p91*
Orange Concept, www.theorangeconcept. com, are a high-standard Dutch venture who offer wakeboarding, waterskiing, parasailing, etc, for all ages and levels of experience.

Also above the water's surface there is **horse riding**, **tennis** and an international grade 18-hole **golf course**.

The **El-Gouna tourist information office**, Downtown, can organize afternoon trips into the nearby desert to sip tea with the local Bedouin and watch the sunset.

Diving

This location provides for the visitor flora and fauna not normally found any further north and gives opportunity for day boats to reach dives normally accessed only by live-aboards. Dives may include the 2 wreck sites as well as the coral gardens and pinnacles. Diving Clubs are all top-notch in terms of safety and eco-consciousness, but are some of the most expensive in Egypt. They also have good snorkelling day trips, mainly to the Dolphin House, Gobal Island or Tawila Island. Among many are:

Blue Brothers Diving Centre, Ocean View Hotel, Abu Tig Marina, T012-321 8025, www.bluebrothersdiving.de.

TGI Diving, Marine Sporting Club, www.tgidiving.com. Open Water course €439 all-in, single day with 2 dives €65.

⊖ Transport

Aïn Sukhna p88

Bus

Buses bound for **Hurghada** will stop if you request them to (though you may have to pay the full Hurghada-bound fare). The frequent buses to/from **Suez** are E£10 and take 1 hr. There are also plenty of microbuses running along the coast between **Suez** and **Hurghada**, just hitch a ride, if there's a seat, they'll stop. Since there's no real bus stop in Sukhna, the police checkpoint south of the Portrait Hotel is a good place to wait if you're trying to get back to Suez or **Cairo**.

El-Gouna p91

Air

Hurghada airport is just 20 km away, with frequent flights from **Cairo** and elsewhere. Taxis from Hurghada airport cost E£60-80, depending on your bargaining skills.

Bus

Local Shuttle buses around El-Gouna cost E£5 for daily ticket and E£15 weekly ticket. Recently imported are some exotic buses from Pakistan to add real colour to the shuttle system, and tuk-tuks run around town for E£5.

Long distance There are several buses commuting between El-Gouna and **Cairo** daily, run by **GoBus** (previously the El-Gouna Transportation Company). Buses bound for El-Gouna leave from the Ramses Hilton in central Cairo and Nasr City at 0730, 1345 and 0045. It's essential to buy your ticket in advance. The ticket booth is next to the **Superjet** sale's counter at Maspiro Mall on the museum side of the Ramses Hilton. Buses bound for **Cairo** leave from Gouna at 0930, 1400, 1630, 1930, 0030. Tickets are E£85-100. Buses to **Hurghada** leave every 20 mins from 0700-2400, E£5. The **High Jet Company** have cheaper less luxurious buses, E£55-65.

Taxi

Taxis running between El-Gouna and **Hurghada** cost E£60-90.

❻ Directory

El-Gouna p91

Medical services El-Gouna Hospital, is world class, T065-3580 012-17, www.elgounahospital.com. There are 3 pharmacies generally open 0900-2100.

Hurghada

People generally end up in Hurghada, 506 km southeast of Cairo, 395 km south of Suez and 269 km northeast of Luxor, for one of three reasons: they've landed an absurdly cheap package tour, they're a diver, or they're stopping off en route between the Sinai and the Nile Valley. In fact, the city is viewed in an ever more disparaging light as increasing numbers of Eastern European package tourists swamp it year-round. Twenty years ago the town centre consisted of one ahwa where fishermen would congregate and a couple of stores; nowadays, hotel developments stretch for 25 km down the coast and the booming real-estate business means there is furious (and hideous) construction of apartment blocks inland. In some ways it is an ideal location for a new tourist development: it is in a virtually uninhabited region, a long way from the Islamic fundamentalist strongholds; the hotels and holiday villages that have been built are largely self-contained, with the exception of fresh water, which is supplied from the Nile Valley; and they employ workers from the major cities. Unfortunately, the area has been developed too quickly since the first constructions in 1992 and frequently without adequate planning controls. However, the beauty of the sea and surrounding mountains is indisputable, some parts of town feel Egyptian in a way that sanitized Na'ama Bay fails to, and (despite the heavy tourist presence) plenty of folk are genuinely friendly and anything goes.

Arriving in Hurghada

Getting there and around Most visitors arrive at Hurghada from the airport, 6 km southwest of the town centre. A taxi to/from town costs E£30-40. Arriving at either bus station (with **Superjet** or **Upper Egypt Bus Co**) you will need to take a short minibus ride unless you plan to stay at the hotels near the Upper Egypt Station. Expect to pay 50 pt-E£1 and possibly 50 pt-E£1 for baggage, especially if it takes up seating. Public transport will drop you in Dahar centre, from where there are microbuses on to Sigala, and then it's another change to get to the Resort Strip.

Dahar is the base for most locals and backpacking travellers, where cheap eats and budget accommodation are found. Two kilometres south, the area known as **Sigala** begins, satiated with mid-range hotels inland and more expensive ones by the seaside. The 'heart' of package-tour Hurghada, the area is filled with restaurants, dive clubs, cafés and nightlife haunts, although this was originally the old fishing village of which just a few old buildings linger on.

Although it is easy to walk around the relatively compact downtown of Dahar it is necessary, when trying to get to the port or the holiday villages to the south of town, to take cheap local buses and minibuses or the town's taxis, which are supposed to use their meters (starting at E£3). Alternatively cars and bicycles can be hired from some of the hotels. Ferries to Sharm El-Sheikh and Duba depart from the port at Sigala's northern tip. Further south, high-end 5-star resorts wind down the coast back to back with no end in sight. The road continues south all the way to the Sudanese border. ▸▸ *See Transport, page 104.*

Information The **tourist office** ⓘ *near the Marine Sports Club, Sharia Bank Misr, Resort Strip, T065-346 3221, open daily 0830-2000.* Also useful are some free publications called the *Red*

Sea Bulletin and *In My Pocket Hurghada*, which can be picked up in hotels and restaurants. **Tourist Police** ① T065-346 3300.

Places in Hurghada

Hurghada (in Arabic, *Al-Ghardaka*) lures visitors with its promise of clear skies, stellar water sports facilities and easy access to diving. A few hotels have coral gardens actually on their site and there are plenty of coral islands offshore from which to study the hidden life below the warm blue waters. However, travellers merely passing through between the Nile Valley and the Sinai will easily be able to fill time, find a cheap hotel with use of a

1 Hurghada

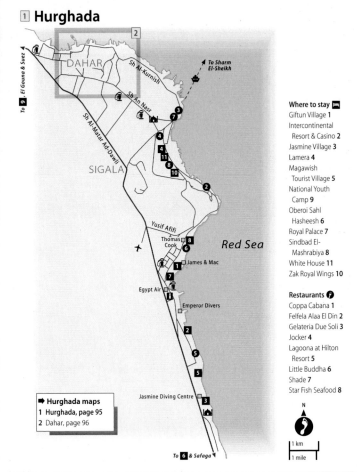

Where to stay
Giftun Village 1
Intercontinental
 Resort & Casino 2
Jasmine Village 3
Lamera 4
Magawish
 Tourist Village 5
National Youth
 Camp 9
Oberoi Sahl
 Hasheesh 6
Royal Palace 7
Sindbad El-
 Mashrabiya 8
White House 11
Zak Royal Wings 10

Restaurants
Coppa Cabana 1
Felfela Alaa El Din 2
Gelateria Due Soli 3
Jocker 4
Lagoona at Hilton
 Resort 5
Little Buddha 6
Shade 7
Star Fish Seafood 8

➡ **Hurghada maps**
1 Hurghada, page 95
2 Dahar, page 96

pool, and have a big night out for not too much money. The *souk* gets even livelier on a Friday with Egyptian shoppers and vendors filling the pavements with their wares. The noise and jostle of people, bikes, cars, bright tacky souvenirs, tired white donkeys, *galabiyas* and veils alongside scantily clad Russian tourists, the smell of *sheesha* pipes, herbs, dead chickens and bad drains assaults all the senses.

If you want to observe a bit of the real life of Hurghada residents, take a stroll around the 'Egyptian areas' in Dahar behind the **Three Corners Empire Hotel** or near 'Ugly Mountain' behind Sharia Abdel Aziz (from which there are great views, sunsets are especially spectacular in the autumn). The housing is pretty crumbly and the streets strewn with litter. Here you will find traditionally dressed women staying at home and scruffy children playing in the streets, boys are bold and loud and girls in *hijabs* wander from school in demure, giggly groups. The old harbour area is an interesting stroll as well, with bright coloured fishing vessels, a vibrant dry dock and small shops catering to locals. There's been a bit of a move to clean up these areas because of the tourists but you can still get a glance of life as it really is in the rest of Egypt.

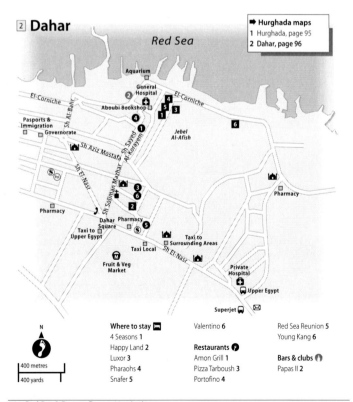

2 **Dahar**

➡ Hurghada maps
1 Hurghada, page 95
2 Dahar, page 96

Where to stay ⊟	Valentino **6**	Red Sea Reunion **5**
4 Seasons **1**		Young Kang **6**
Happy Land **2**	**Restaurants ⊘**	
Luxor **3**	Amon Grill **1**	**Bars & clubs ⊘**
Pharaohs **4**	Pizza Tarboush **3**	Papas II **2**
Snafer **5**	Portofino **4**	

The **Marine Museum** ① *daily 0800-2000, E£10 for the museum and its adjacent aquarium*, is about 6 km to the north of the town centre and is associated with the National Institute of Oceanography and Fisheries. A good place to begin learning about the marine life of the area with stuffed examples of coral reef fish, shark, manta rays and associated birdlife as well as samples of coral and shells. The **Aquarium** ① *daily 0900-2200, E£10, on Sharia El-Corniche near the hospital*, is quite small but has live specimens in well-marked tanks. It may be worth a visit if you are not a diver, though a glass-bottomed boat is much more of an experience for E£50.

Hurghada islands, reefs & dive sites

Not to scale

↘ Dive sites

1 Abu Ramada North
2 Abu Ramada South
   (The Aquarium)
3 Careless Reef
4 El Aruk
5 El Fanadir
6 Erg Abu Ramada
7 Erg Sabina
8 Erg Somaya
9 Fanous East
10 Fanous West
11 Giftun Police
12 Gota Abu Ramada
13 Little Giftun
14 Sha'ab Disha
15 Sha'ab Eshta
16 Sha'ab Farasha
17 Sha'ab Sabina
18 Sha'ab Tiffany
19 Sha'ab Torf
20 Sha'ab Rur
21 Stone Beach
22 Turtle Bay
23 Um Gamar North
24 Um Gamar South

Dive sites

Among the best dive sites are **Um Gamar**, 1½ hours north, a plateau of beautiful soft and hard corals with a good drop-off and cave. Also has a kingdom of poisonous snakes. Dives are made onto a slope that drops gradually from 15 m to 76 m. **Sha'ab Al-Erg** is 1½ hours north. There's a coral plateau including table coral and, if you are lucky, manta rays and dolphins. At the **Careless Reef** you may see shark. There is a spectacular drop-off and ergs. This site is for advanced divers only, due to the currents. The island stands over three columns of rare corals resting originally on a 10- to 15-m surface. **Giftun Islands** are close to Hurghada and thus very popular, and fast deteriorating. Fortunately they possess a number of reefs still teeming with plenty of fish including moray eels. **El-Fanadir**, is a popular site close to Hurghada with a pretty reef wall and drop-off with nice soft corals. **Sha'ab Abu Ramada**, 40 minutes south, with a good drop-off, has lots of fish and coral. Usually a drift dive. The corals shapes are unique: round and brain-like. Nearby **Gota Abu Ramada**, is nicknamed the 'Aquarium' due to the abundance of marine life among the mountainous coral garden, including butterfly fish, snappers, and banner fish. Further afield are a series of islands including **Shadwan**, **Tawlah** and **Gubal**, around which there are chances of seeing pelagic fish and dolphins.

Beaches and etiquette

There are **public beaches** ① *E£7-10, depending on services*, in Dahar near the Three Corners Empire, around the Port at Sigala and after the V-junction on Sharia Sheraton Sigala. At all three, and in particular the first two it is unacceptable to wear a bathing costume or less. Women sit in a proper manner on upright chairs and if they do venture into the sea, they are fully clothed. Men can wear shorts.

If you are not staying at a hotel with beach access, the only option is to pay to use one of the resorts' beaches. This costs between E£50-100 daily.

Excursions from Hurghada

By boat A recommended trip is to **Mahmya Island**, about one hour off the coast of Hurghada, which has a gorgeous beach, some good snorkelling and a restaurant. It's also possible to take a trip further afield to Tobia Island, in Safaga Bay, with its sandy lagoons and untouched (for how long?) corals surrounded by turquoise water. There's also a sea cruise via Shedwan Island, the Gulf of Suez, and even Ras Mohammed (see page 36). The trip takes at least six hours and costs about E£250 – check with local travel guides. These trips do not run every day, but according to demand.

By land Day trips visit the Roman ruins of **Mons Claudianus** near Jebel Fatira (1355 m), the largest and best-preserved site in the Eastern Desert. There's evidence here of Roman military presence, a penal colony, a Roman road and columns as well as a Roman settlement with houses, stable and the fortress of Om Dikhal. It's also a quarry and you can see the remains of the cells used to house the workers/prisoners who quarried the stone, some of which made its way to Rome in barges where it formed the pillars in the portico of the Pantheon.

Mons Porphyritis, 55 km northwest of Hurghada at the foot of Jebel Abu Dukhan (1641 m), has some ruinous remains of a Roman temple to Serapis and ancient quarries for porphyry, a popular stone used for sarcophagi and facing walls. To visit the two Roman sites, you will need to hire a car for at least a half-day.

⦿ Hurghada listings

For sleeping and eating price codes and other relevant information, see pages 11-15.

▣ Where to stay

Hurghada *p94, maps p95 and p96*
There are as many officially registered hotels in Hurghada as there are non-registered ones – and new ones springing up all the time. Although most visitors pre-book their accommodation as part of a package with their flight there should be no problem, except perhaps during the winter high season, for independent travellers to find a room. Like everywhere in Egypt, prices change, sometimes drastically, depending on the number of tourists, so treat these prices as variable. Single female travellers should be on guard when staying at budget hotels.

€€€€ Magawish Swiss Inn Resort, Resort Strip, T065-346 4620-9, www.swiss inn.net. 425 rooms, good standard, private bay and beach to south of port, offers all the normal facilities plus a wide range of water sports and children's activities.

€€€€ Oberoi Sahl Hasheesh, Sahl Hasheesh, T065-344 0777, www.oberoi hotels.com. Truly luxurious and utterly exclusive, miles away from the mass tourism of Hurghada in both mood and geography, this is the top choice for those who can afford it. An all-suite resort, built in the domed Moorish style, all columns, arches and striped facades, from the sunken marble baths you can see the sea or the walled gardens. The pools are sublime as is the private beach, and the spa receives high praise.

€€€ Giftun Beach Resort, Sharia Youseff Afifi, Resort Strip, T065-346 3040, www.giftun beachresort.com. Comfortable bungalows set in a vast private sandy beach, 8 km from town at the start of the resort strip. Pool, squash, tennis and all watersports are free except diving (**James & Mac** dive centre on site is recommended), windsurfing and tennis lessons. Main restaurant provides buffet meals and there are bars and discos. A good choice.

€€€ Living With Art, the German Consulate, 465 El-Gabal El-Shamali, Sigala, T065-344 5734, T012-211 8338, www.living withart.biz. 18 modern apartments of varying sizes and layouts, all uniquely decorated, with large bathrooms, several balconies, warm lighting and decor and specially designed wrought-iron furniture. From the rooftop (with bar, spa, jacuzzi, pergolas and loungers) there are amazing views down the hill over town and sea. Karin is a simply wonderful cook, evenings are spent drinking German beer in her homely kitchen, and you'll forget you are in Hurghada the moment you enter the tranquil courtyard of bougainvillea. And at €50 per person half-board, it is excellent value for such a unique place.

€€€ Royal Palace Hotel, Sigala, T065-346 3660, www.royalpalacehotel.com. 120 rooms, private beach, 3 restaurants, good food. With a good diving centre and easy access to the beach for disabled people, this is one of the most reliable hotels in Hurghada, despite being slightly tacky.

€€€ Sindbad El-Mashrabiya, Resort Strip, T065-344 3330/2, www.sindbad-group.com. A pleasant Moorish-style hotel with 3 pools, plenty of excellent watersport facilities and its own private beach. This is where the yellow **Sindbad Submarine** trips are based.

€€€ Three Corners Empire Hotel, Sharia Sayed Korrayem, Dahar, T065-354 9200/9, www.threecorners.com. Part of the Triton hotels chain, this domineering block in Dahar is always busy with package tourists and is a reliable mid-range choice. There's an unspectacular pool, plenty of bars and bazaars and a handy location in the thick of Downtown.

€€ Luxor Hotel, Sharia Mustashfa, Dahar, T065-354 2877, www.luxorhotel-eg.com. Relatively new place, rooms here are more comfortable than most in this price range and bathrooms clean. Set back from the main road, it's a quiet if anonymous choice. There's a small front terrace, and discounts for longer stays. Guests can use the beach/pool a nearby hotel.

€€ Zak Royal Wings Hotel, Sigala, T065-344 6012, www.zakhotel.com. All rooms have views on to the small central swimming pool and the standard amenities you would expect for the price. Everything is painted white giving an almost Mediterranean air, the **Rossi** restaurant serves decent Italian food, adjacent **Papas Bar** is famed, and the location set back from the road is in its favour. A small and pleasant hotel.

€€-€ White Albatros, 162 Sharia Sheraton, Sigala, T065-344 2519, walbatros53@ hotmail.com. Very clean hotel in the upper range of the budget category, and worth paying the extra for cheerful white rooms with green paintwork and decent bathrooms. British management, rooms with bath. Fridge, TV, a/c and balconies on the upper floors have seaviews. Popular with long-staying guests, there's a nice rooftop with loungers and downstairs coffee shop.

€ 4 Seasons Hotel, off Sharia Sayed al-Korayem, Dahar, T/F065-354 4201, T012-7143 917, forseasonhurghda@hotmail.com. Rooms are clean if scruffy, all with balconies, fans or a/c, some bathrooms are very poky. Use of the pool at the **Geisum Village** is a bonus, as is the roof terrace. Recommended among others in the budget category, has a more backpacker vibe and runs cheap snorkelling trips to Giftun Island. Breakfast included.

€ Gobal, Sharia Sheikh Sabak, Dahar, T065-354 6623. Small very cheap rooms, all with bathrooms outside, are do-able if you're on a real budget. You won't see any other foreigners here, sheets are clean and staff pleasant.

€ Lamera Hotel, Sharia Sheraton, Sigala, T065-344 2075. Large clean rooms are nothing special and paintwork is grubby, but it's a convenient location mid-way along Sigala's main drag. Rooms have all the amenities you'd expect, TV, fridge, a/c, and there is access to a beach (about 10 mins' walk). Get a room high up at the front for sea views.

€ Pharaohs, off Sharia Sayed El-Korayem, Dahar. Rooms vary in quality, best are on top floor where a sea view is available. A little gloomy but close to the action and has a small garden at the front. Breakfast costs E£10.

€ Snafer Hotel, off Sharia Sayed al-Korayem, Dahar, T/F065-354 0260, snafer_hurghada_hotel@hotmail.com. Decent-sized plain rooms all have fridge, a/c and balcony. The large soft beds and clean white linen are a real mark up from most of the budget places, as are the bathrooms, and compensate for a slightly higher price. There's no lift, which is a bit of a killer for the upper rooms (some of which have sea views). For breakfast pay E£10.

€ St George Hotel, off Sharia El-Nasr, Dahar, T065-354 8246. Rooms are certainly musty, gloomy and shabby, but have clean sheets, fans, and there's a roof view. Only the rooms with shared bath have balconies, while the Christian family that own it are kind.

€ Valentino Hotel, Sharia El-Corniche, Dahar, T010-620 2182. Small, friendly and spotless this is a good choice that has mid-range facilities for almost budget prices. Freshly painted rooms (a/c, satellite TV) and public spaces. There's a popular and laid-back terrace coffee shop (with alcohol) and a cute restaurant for breakfast. Staff are very polite.

🍴 Restaurants

Hurghada *p94, maps p95 and p96*

Good restaurants in Hurghada are as plentiful as good hotels. Many of the cheaper ones are in Dahar, with a few in Sigala. If you feel extravagant head to the new Marina Blvd area for great Thai, Spanish and other international cuisine. A bigger beach and pool have been created here, and with the absence of cars it's a relaxing spot during the day – perfect for children – and then comes alive at night.

€€€ Lagoona, at Hilton Resort, T065-346 5036. Open daily 1930-2330. A fish restaurant and international dishes. Open aspect gives breathtaking views.

€€€ Little Buddha, next to Sindbad Club, Village Rd, Resort Strip, T065-345 0120, www.littlebuddha-hurghada.com. Cocktails, great sushi and Pacific cuisine can be sampled on the 1st-floor seating area under the gaze of a giant gold Buddha. Food served from 1600. Turns into a club later on.

€€€ Shade, Marina Blvd, Sigala. Swedish-owned, this restaurant-bar has a Norwegian chef and everything on the menu is grilled and fresh. The salmon steak is tremendous, frequented by Hurghada's ex-pats.

€€€-€€ La Luna, Sharia Sheraton, Sigala, T065-344 8691-3. Open 24 hrs. Generic Italian restaurant making an attempt at contemporary decor, some outdoor seating, and very popular for its excellent pizzas and vast menu.

€€€-€€ Scruples Billiardeni, Sharia Abdel Azizi Mostafa, Dahar, T065-354 4796, www.scruples-reasea.com. Open 0900-0100. Classy it ain't, but if you fancy a steak or vaguely French cooking in an unpretentious place, head here. The outdoor chairs by a market square also make a good location for a beer.

€€ Cacao Bar, Sharia Sayed al-Korayem/Hospital St, Dahar, T012-6184 861. Pretty good Italian food, the pizzas are recommended. It's also a popular drinking hole, see page 101, open 24 hrs.

€€ El-Joker Fish Restaurant, Midan Sheraton, Sigala, T065-344 3146. Has a long-standing reputation. Pick your own fish, pay by weight, or choose from the extensive menu of 'meals'. A no-frills kind of fish joint, don't be put off by the exterior, the environment improves as you ascend the stairs.

€€ Felfela Alaa El Din, Sharia Sheraton, Dahar T065-344 2411. Offers modestly priced authentic Egyptian food, overlooking the sea, a little out of the town centre, north of the resort strip, but worth it for the view and the food.

€€ Red Sea Reunion, Sharia Sayed al-Korayem/Hospital St, Dahar, T012-719 6267, www.redsearunion.com. In its heyday, this was about the only restaurant with a rooftop terrace and hence always packed out. Not so now, but the rooftop remains relaxing and pleasant both day and night, offering Italian, Indian, fish and steaks. They have Nubian music on Wed nights, and a relatively low-key DJ on other nights, and the staff are genuinely friendly. Free Wi-Fi.

€€ Rossi Pizzeria, Zak Wings Hotel, Sharia Sheraton, Sigala, T065-344 7676. Traditional Italian cuisine and sandwiches with a decent salad bar.

€€ Star Fish Seafood Restaurant, Sharia Sheraton, Sigala, T065-344 3751. Open 1200-0100. Excellent value for grilled, fried or baked fish, fabulous shrimps and the salads are some of the best around for only E£3. A large clean functional place, busy at all hours, they also home deliver. There is a new branch in the Senzo Mall.

€ For passable *koshari*, try the joint on Sharia El-Nassr to the left of the Upper Egypt bus station.

Ahwas and cafés

Authentic local *ahwas* are in Dahar. There are a number by the small mosque in the centre. Strictly speaking they're generally patronized by local men only, but with so many foreigners around, few take offence if visitors enjoy a *sheesha* or a cup of tea and gaze at the world on the streets around you. There are also numerous tourist cafés including those mentioned here as restaurants and bars. Try the sugar cane juice E£1, fresh orange E£5, or whatever fruit is in season, at the best juice shop in Hurghada on Sharia Sayyed, next to **Supermarket Rashidy**.

Coppa Cabana, Sharia Sheraton, Sigala, T012-796 3653. Gorgeous home-made Italian ice cream, plus coffee that's the real-deal, this cute corner café never disappoints. They also have a new place at the Marina Blvd,

Gelateria Due Soli. It is more about the gelati than the coffee.

Miramar, Mohamady Hwedak St, T065-345 0920. An upmarket coffee shop frequented more by wealthy Egyptians than package tourists. Dark red interiors with striped Moorish arches, Orientalist prints on the walls, and comfy indoor and terrace seating, you soon forget the ugly main road outside when puffing on one of the best *sheeshas* in town.

🍸 Bars and nightclubs

Hurghada *p94, maps p95 and p96*

At the last count there were over 100 bars in Hurghada. As a major tourist resort there is less worry about offending Islamic sensibilities. Besides the main hotel restaurants, which feature discos and serve alcohol, there are a few clubs in town. There are plenty of belly-dancing shows at all the big hotels on a nightly basis, mostly performed by Russian women.

Cacao Bar, Sharia Sayed al-Korayem/Hospital St, Dahar, T012-6184 861. Open 24 hrs and always has a few drinkers whatever the time, happy hours daily 1500-1800, free Wi-Fi, and occasional live music. The pizzas aren't bad.

HedKandi, Marina Blvd. A chilled-out vibe by the sea, during the day it's a pleasant spot to relax on the beach then it transforms at night-time into a rocking disco, plus they have excellent full-moon parties.

Little Buddha, next to **Sindbad Resort**, Village Rd, Resort Strip, T065-345 0120, www.littlebuddha-hurghada.com. Open 2330-0400. The coolest place to go out and many rate it as the best club in Hurghada.

Ministry of Sound, Papas Beach Club, T016-883 3550, www.ministryofsound egypt.com, Sigala. A proper night out, with good music, and the place is usually packed. Resident and guest DJs from Europe, as you'd expect from the Ministry the music gets everyone going 7 nights a week.

Peanuts Bar, Sharia, Dahar. Open from 1200-0200. Copious amounts of peanuts available to supplement copious amounts of beer, a happening spot with package tourists from the nearby Three Corners. Free Wi-Fi and sports events shown on big screens.

O Shopping

Hurghada *p94, maps p95 and p96*

Hurghada has few local shops, although all the major hotels and holiday villages have arcades that cater for tourists' requirements. Souvenir stands are plentiful. T-shirts, towels, carpets, jewellery, scarabs, *sheesha* pipes, papyrus, pyramids, stuffed camels – the list is endless. If buying gold or silver make sure it's stamped and you get a certificate of authenticity. Remember trade in coral and some animals and fish is illegal. Herbs here are cheaper than at home, but if your travels will take you beyond Hurghada, better deals exist elsewhere. Duty-free goods can be bought at the Pyramid at the roundabout in Sigala and next to the **Royal Palace** and **Ambassador** hotels. Bear in mind that passport stamps for duty- free are only valid for 2 days. There is a **Metro** super-market on Sharia Sheraton and Sharia An-Nasr, and **Abu Ashara supermarket** on Sharia Sheraton. The local fruit and veg market is near Al-Dahar Sq, beyond Sharia El-Nasr. If you are travelling further south this is your last chance to stock up on products such as contact lens solution, tampons and hair conditioner.

Bookshops

Al Ahram, in Esplanada Mall, south of Sigala. Open 0900-2200.

Pyramid Bookshop, in Jasmine Village. With international newspapers.

Red Sea Bookstores, Zabargad Mall, Sharia Al-Hadaba, www.redseabookstores.com. Open 1100-2300. Has the best selection of books in Hurghada.

⚠ What to do

Hurghada *p94, maps p95, p96 and p97*

Boat trips

All-day boat excursions go to Giftun Island, in the bay, which has a nice beach and good snorkelling even though it gets overcrowded. It's easy to join a boat from any of the cheap hotels or from the marina for €25, expect your tour to include a fish barbecue. To just visit the island for a couple of hours is €15. For around €400, you can rent a private boat from the port or the athletic marine club for a day.

Some operators (including **Flying Dolphin Sea Trips**, **Nefertiti Diving Centre** and **Sunshine Sea Trips**) also organize longer boat trips, such as 3-day trips to Gobal Island, overnight excursions to Giftun, and expeditions to the deeper reefs, such as the House of Sharks (20 km south) where experienced divers can see hammerheads, tiger sharks and other exotic marine life.

To view the underwater world and keep dry there is the Finnish-built a/c 44-seater **Sindbad Submarine**, T065-344 4688, offering a 2-hr roundtrip (about 50 mins underwater). Book the day before. Transfer by boat to submarine (30 mins), which goes down to 22 m with diver in front attracting fish with food (not a recommended procedure). Trips leave daily 1000-1200, adults US$50, children under 12 US$25.

Sailing boats are available. Catamarans and toppers are best found at windsurf schools. Glass-bottomed boats are available at most hotels for about E£50 per hr per person.

Diving in Hurghada – tales and tips

- If you want to get any qualifications make sure your instructor can speak your mother tongue. You can't be safe if you cannot understand the instructor. Be careful in choosing your dive centre – safety, environmental impact and price should be on your agenda. Bargain-basement prices could mean that short cuts are being made.
- Make sure you are insured to dive.
- Fly-by-night operators do exist. Always be on your guard. Go to an approved operator and watch out for scams, eg non-PADI centres flying PADI flags.
- The best options are those centres that have regular guests on dive holidays flying in from abroad.
- Common tricks include: cheap deals, making you feel guilty or rude if you refuse, sudden loss of understanding of your language, free desert/restaurant trips, offers of marriage! Also talk of donations to the decompression chamber, Sinai National Parks and Giftun Islands – these are virtually all compulsory and it is the diver that pays. (The government has introduced a US$1 a day charge for the decompression chamber and a US$2 tax for the Giftun Island Reef.)
- HEPCA (Hurghada Environmental Protection and Conservation Association), www.hepca.com, is concerned about environmental destruction. It organizes cleanups at various Red Sea sites. Some dive centres are members, but this is not necessarily a guarantee of safety.
- Membership of the Red Sea Diving and Watersport Association and the Egyptian Underwater Sports Association is not proof of safety either. Membership is a requirement of law.
- Contact PADI, BSAC, CMAS and SSI while at home for advice.
- Check whether dive centres will pick you up or if you will have to arrange your own transport.
- The sale of shells and coral is illegal, and large fines and long prison sentences can result if you are successfully prosecuted. Removing anything living or dead from the water in Protected Areas is forbidden. Fishermen are banned from these areas. Continuing to plunder the marine environment will cause permanent damage.

Desert trips

It's become easy to arrange day trips to the desert from most tour operators/hotels, to get a sense of the endless expanses surrounding the city and a chance to have a bit of a Bedouin 'camp' experience. Expect to pay about €35 for a quad bike, €25 per person for a place in a jeep, or €50-60 for 2 people in a buggy.

Diving

Though the rapid development of tourist sites and the actions of thoughtless divers keen to take a piece of the Red Sea home has yielded tragic destruction in the reefs around Hurghada, the area still boasts some of the best diving in the world. The waters are warm year-round, visibility is always good, and currents are mild. In addition to a wide variety of coral, vast schools of sparkling tiny fish and large pelagic swimmers along the seabed's deep walls, you may have the chance to swim with dolphins, hammerheads and manta rays.

Below is a selection of the better diving clubs. All teach accredited dive courses and offer live-aboard safaris to nearby sites, daily and extended trips. Shop around a bit before you commit, make sure you can get on with your dive instructor and that s/he speaks your language. Choose with care, check the qualifications, see what safety precautions are in place. Cheap may not be best.

Colona Divers, in **Magawish Swiss Inn Resort**, Resort Strip, T010-213 8409, www.colona.com.

Diver's Lodge, at **Intercontinental Resort**, Resort Strip, T065-346 5100, www.divers-lodge.com.

Emperor Divers, Hilton Plaza, T065-344 4854, www.emperordivers.com, with branches all over the Red Sea they come highly recommended.

James and Mac, Giftun Beach Resort, T065-346 2141, www.james-mac.com. Good reputation.

Fishing
An International Fishing Festival takes place every Feb. Spear fishing is illegal in the Red Sea.
Marine Sports Club, next to the **Grand Hotel**, T065-346 3004.

Snorkelling
Boats with motors to tow or for fishing or snorkelling are for hire. **Three Corners**, **Shedwan** and **Coral Beach** hotels all have house reefs, but the best reefs are offshore. With a tour, a day's snorkelling, including lunch, costs from €25-40. Good snorkelling sites include Giftun Islands, Fanadir, Um Gamar, and Mahmya island.

Tour operators and travel agents
Besides the independent travel agents there is at least one in each major hotel. With the Nile Valley only a few hours away, many travel agencies organize day-long tours to Luxor that depart Hurghada in the early morning convoy and return in the evening.
Misr Travel, Sigala, T065-344 2131.
Thomas Cook, 3 Sharia El-Nasr, Dahar, T065-354 1870. Main office for tourist

facilities. Also a branch with financial services in Sigala, at 8 Sharia Sheraton.

Windsurfing
Windsurfing is particularly good thanks to the gusty winds, usually 4-8 on Beaufort Scale. Many hotels offer equipment but much of it is outdated. The best equipment is found at centres offering windsurf holiday packages. Ensure your choice of centre has a rescue boat that works.
Happy Surf, www.happy-surf.de have branches at the **Hilton Plaza** and Sofitel (German-run). Expect to pay about €150 per hr, more for kiteboards.
Planet Windsurf, www.planetwindsurf.com, British-based company; also do kiteboarding.

Transport

Hurghada *p94, maps p95 and p96*

Air
International flights go to and from all over Europe. There are 2 or 3 daily flights from Hurghada to **Cairo**. Flights also go direct to **Aswan**, **Sharm El-Sheikh** and **Alexandria**. Times and numbers of flights change daily so it is best to visit **EgyptAir** in person or go online, as the phones are rarely answered. Flights to Cairo and Sharm El-Sheikh are approximately E£300.

Airlines EgyptAir, www.egyptair.com, in the square with the new mosque and a branch on Sharia Sheraton, T065-346 3034-7. Open 0800-2000.

Bus
Local Minibus and microbuses make regular circuits of Dahar. Dahar–Sigala should cost E£1.
Long distance The main bus station is on Sharia El-Nassr in Dahar from where **Upper Egypt** buses leave. Further down the street to the south are the **GoBus** and **Superjet** offices. **High Jet**, T065-344 9700, have an office near the police station in Sigala.

Upper Egypt, T065-354 7582, runs regular daily buses north to **Suez** (every hr, 0600-2400; 5 hrs; E£35) and **Cairo** (11 per day; 6-7 hrs, between E£50-70 depending on time of departure). There are 6 buses per day southeast to **Luxor** (5 hrs; E£30), via **Qena**, 2 of which carry on to **Aswan** (8 hrs). Buses to **El-Quesir** (2 hrs, E£25) via **Safaga** (E£5-7) leave at 0100, 0300, 0500 and 2000, carrying on to **Marsa Alam** (4 hrs, E£35) and **Shalatein** (E£50, 9 hrs).

Superjet, Sharia Al-Nasr, T065-355 3499, runs 4 daily buses to **Cairo** at 1200, 1430, 1700 and 2400 (6 hrs, E£70); the 1430 goes on to **Alexandria** (9 hrs, E£90).

GoBus (previously called El-Gouna Transport), Sharia Al-Nasr, T065-355 6199, T19567, runs 17 daily buses to **Cairo** (via **El-Gouna**) 6 hrs, E£45-150 depending on class of bus (the 1430 is cheapest).

Many of the buses to and from Cairo are genuinely 'lux', with a/c and plastic still covering the seats, and therefore more expensive. It's wise to check schedules south to Marsa Alam as they fluctuate seasonally, and a good idea to book a ticket a day in advance if you are going to Luxor, Aswan or Alexandria.

Car

Most car rental agencies are scattered around Sharia Sheraton.

Ferry

High-speed a/c ferry to **Sharm El-Sheikh** on the Sinai Peninsula (1½ hrs, though weather can impact duration), booking is essential from **Red Sea Jet**, office on the Sharia Sheraton in front of Pacha resort, T065-344 9481/2, or through a travel agent such as **Thomas Cook**, Sharia El Nasr, Dahar, T065-354 1870, or **Spring Tours**, Sharia Sheraton, Sigala, T065-344 2150. 1-way fare costs E£250, return E£450. Ferries leave Hurghada for Sharm El-Sheikh at 0900 on Sat, Tue and Thu and at 0400 on Mon. They depart from Sharm El-Sheikh back to Hurghada on the same days at 1700, or 1800 on Mon.

There are also 3 weekly ferry services to **Duba**, in Saudi Arabia (3 hrs, departs 1000 but you should be in the port at 0800, E£325, more if you have a car). Contact **Sheriff Tours**, at Sand Beach, T065-345 5147, to book a ticket or for more information.

Taxi

Local Minimum charge E£5-10 within Dahar. To get to **Sigala** from Dahar, E£15-20.

Long distance Service taxis operate to destinations south, north and west, although as a foreigner you may have to be insistent to join those travelling to the Nile Valley or south to Marsa Alam (lone travellers or couples stand a better chance). You need to go to the service taxi station across the roundabout from the Telephone Centrale. Service taxi fares are approx E£5 to **Safaga** (1 hr), E£20 to **Marsa Alam** (3 hrs), E£50 to **Cairo** (5-7 hrs), E£25 to **Suez** (4 hrs). You may have to wait some time for the car to fill up (7 people, microbus 14). If you're in a rush, you can pay for empty seats in order to leave sooner. For long distances, fares and travel times are less than the bus but it's more dangerous as drivers often speed quite fearlessly.

❶ Directory

Hurghada *p94, maps p95 and p96*
Immigration Passports and Immigration Office: Sharia El-Nasr, north of town, Sat-Thu 0800-1400, T065-354 6727. **Medical services** International Hospital, El-Ahya, T065-355 3785, **El-Salam Hospital**, Sigala, T065-354 8785-7, **General Hospital**, Sharia Aziz Mostafa, T065-354 6740. The best hospital is in El-Gouna, **El-Gouna Hospital**, T065-3580012-7, www.elgounahospital.com.eg, where there is also a decompression chamber; decompression chamber also in Hurghada at the **Naval Hospital**, T065-344 9150.

South of Hurghada

Until the 1980s, the coast south of Hurghada was virtually untouched by tourism and a wealth of coral reefs and islands lay undisturbed but by the adventurous few. Recent years have seen a boom in hotel building, and large resorts pepper the coast between El-Quseir and Marsa Alam as an airport brings in package tourists mainly from Germany and Italy. Yet the port of El-Quseir remains a peaceful little place, with accommodation suiting backpackers and a unique atmosphere, while south of Marsa Alam restrictions imposed to protect the environment mean that new hotels have to be eco-friendly and hence there are some truly stunning getaways if you have the time and the money. The interior of the Eastern Desert remains one of Egypt's least explored areas, hiding ancient tribes and scattered ruins in the mountainous expanses stretching towards Sudan.

Safaga

Safaga stands 567 km from Cairo, 65 km (45 minutes by taxi) south of Hurghada's airport, where the coastal road meets the main road across the Eastern Desert to Qena. Though the town isn't particularly beautiful, it has this stretch of the Red Sea's usual attractions: diving, snorkelling and perhaps the most famous wind on the coast. The stiff breezes that favoured the trading vessels along these shores now provide excellent conditions for kite- and windsurfing, generally cross-shore in the morning and side-shore in the early afternoon. The Windsurfing World Championships have been held here in the past. There are a few large resort hotels in Safaga, and the proximity of the beautiful sandbank island of Tobia and the lagoon at Ras Abu Soma give the option of easy day-trips. Safaga has also gained a reputation as a health tourism destination, with many psorisis and arthritis sufferers journeying from afar to roast in the mineral-enriched black sands. With such geological riches, the area does not rely totally on tourism. It has local phosphate mines that export the mineral overseas.

Most travellers simply pass through in a convoy on their way between Hurghada and the Nile Valley. Outside of the sea, there is very little to visit other than a small fort that overlooks the town and offers good views.

El-Quseir

Further south is El-Quseir, 650 km from Cairo and 140 km south of Hurghada, an old Roman encampment and once a busy port. Far enough away from the hoards of package tourists in Hurghada and Safaga, and without any mega-resorts such as are found on the stretch of coast south to Marsa Alam, the small sleepy town has managed to retain a lot of its ancient charm. Coral-block houses with creaky wooden balconies are dotted around the old village by the seafront, people are incredibly friendly and move at a slower pace. The surroundings are still pristine and the nearby snorkelling and diving superb, but the town's real charm lies in the unspoilt continuity of real life – something that's missing from other more user-friendly beach retreats in Sinai and the Red Sea. The sense of history and sea-trade, the tangible presence of Islam (heightened by the noise of 33 mosques) and the narrow pastel-toned streets make it feel like an Egyptian version of Zanzibar. But considerably smaller and with fewer tourists.

The name 'Quseir' means 'short' as this was the starting point both of the shortest sea-route to Mecca and the shortest way to the Nile Valley, five days away overland by camel. Located in a small inlet sheltered by a coral reef, the modern road inland from El-Quseir to Qift, just south of Qena, follows an ancient pharaonic route that is lined with forts, built at a time when almost 100 small but very rich gold mines operated in the region. It was from El-Quseir that Queen Hatshepsut departed on her famous expedition to the Land of Punt and throughout the pharaonic era there was trade with Africa in wild animals, to supply the pharaohs with elephants during times of warfare. This was also once the most important Muslim port on the Red Sea. In the 10th century it was superseded first by Aydhab, which is the ancient name for the Halaib in the currently disputed triangle on the Egyptian/Sudanese border, and then by Suez after the canal was opened in 1869. Now the port's main function revolves around the export of phosphates. The 16th-century fortress of Sultan Selim (rebuilt by the French in 1798) still dominates the town centre and creates a mystique that no other Red Sea village quite has.

Places in El-Quseir The partly ruined **fortress** ① *E£15, students E£8, 0800-1700 daily except during Fri prayers, incorporates an excellent visitor centre,* was built in 1571 by Sultan Selim to protect the Nile Valley from attacks from the sea and to shield pilgrims bound for Mecca from Bedouin raids. The devoted left their camels and horses at the fort while they made the *hajj*. There was conflict here at the end of the 18th century – during the French campaign, and then again between the British Indian Army coming in from Bombay and the Egyptian campaign to the Arabian Peninsula headed by Ibrahim Pasha in 1816. The central watchtower affords good views of the surprisingly high mountain ranges to the south, which contain the mineral wealth of the area; from here the sea and mountains were surveyed for invaders.

Other buildings from this earlier period include the mosques of Al-Faroah, Abdel-Rehim Al-Qenay and Al-Sanussi and the fabulous derelict granary just behind the old police station. There are also a significant number of tombs, mainly near the fortress and Corniche, of holy men who died en route to Mecca, which are still considered important by the town's inhabitants. To the north of town, the compound of the old Italian phosphate mining works contains derelict warehouses, an ornate modern church and a tiny crumbling 'museum' containing a few mouldering stuffed animals, reptiles and birds (someone will appear with the key). Nearby is a small but colourful fruit and vegetable market.

Wadi Hammamat About 100 km along en route to Qift, Wadi Hammamat has some 200 examples of pharaonic graffiti – hieroglyphic inscriptions – in the cliff, including the names of Pepi, Sesostris, Seti, Cambyses and Darius. The inscriptions lie along an ancient trade route where remains of old wells and watch towers are also detectable.

Marsa Shagra

This remote bay, 113 km south of El-Quseir and 13 km north of Marsa Alam, has transformed into a small village celebrated by divers. There is an extensive underwater cave system to explore, and some outstanding coral formations. It's also near a group of striking offshore reefs with great sloping walls, the mysterious **Elphinstone Reef** among them, where in its dark depths some say lie the remains of an unknown pharaoh. (See page 115).

Marsa Alam

Once merely a tiny fishing village 130 km south of El-Quseir, Marsa Alam is developing fast, with a new mall being built to the south of town. Nevertheless, the surrounding area (if not the town itself) remains a gem of the southern coast. Marsa Alam is also a way station between the Nile Valley and the Red Sea since a road through the Eastern desert connects it to Edfu, 250 km to the west. The small harbour is nestled in a beautiful area where the coast is lined with mangrove swamps that encourage rich bird and marine life. These mangroves are protected and all new developments are supposed to be eco-conscious in order to ensure the preservation of the fragile environment. There is nowhere to stay in the town itself, and the coast north to El-Quseir is dotted with Disney-esque resorts that make an astonishing spectacle lit up at night. Independent travellers are usually heading south of Marsa Alam to one of the smaller camps at Tondoba Bay, Marsa Nakari, Wadi Lahami or Wadi Gimal. It is not a particularly welcoming town and has no discernible centre, save for the bus station. There is also very little public transport and most of the resorts or camps are spread along the coast. A taxi is needed to get around, and it is best to try not to arrive late at night without a reservation somewhere. ▶▶ For dive sites, see page 115.

Berenice

A very ancient city named by Ptolemy II, Berenice became a trading port around 275 BC. The ruined temple of **Semiramis** is near the modern town. Inland there are remains of the emerald mines of Wadi Sakait that were worked from pharaonic to Roman times. Berenice is noted for both quantity and quality of fish and having a climate reputed to promote good health. The coast is lined with mangrove swamps and there are some beautiful coves that are completely isolated. However, it is extremely unlikely you would be able to visit the town as the police are particularly uncooperative here. The nearest you will probably get is on a live-aboard dive boat.

Offshore is the **Zabargad**, a most unusual volcanic island. Evidence of its origin is found in the (olive-green) olivine mined as a semi-precious gem stone. Mining has been active here on and off since 1500 BC. **Peridot Hill** (named after another semi-precious stone) offers breathtaking views of the surrounding area. A wonderful place to watch the dolphins and, in season, the migrating birds. Once off limits to visitors, Zabargad Island has finally been declared a Protected Marine Park by the Egyptian government. Sometimes a permit is required for this area, though a bit of *baksheesh* to the right people can often grant access. It is still relatively untouristed and safari boats spend three to four days exploring the dive sites and surrounds.

Excursions inland There is one interesting excursion possible from here into the interior, but a guide is essential. The tomb and mosque of **Sidi Abul Hassan Al-Shazli** lies some distance inland. The buildings are modern, being last restored on the instructions of King Farouk after his visit in 1947. The road is a distance of 110 km southwards off the main road west towards Edfu. Al-Shazli (1196-1258) was an influential Sufi sheikh originally from the northwest of Africa but who spent much of his life in Egypt. He had a large and important following and was noted for his piety and unselfishness. He travelled annually to Mecca, for which Marsa Alam was convenient. His *moulid* is popular despite the isolation of the site, attracting around 20,000 devotees. Events stretch over the 10 days before Eid Al-Adha, and if you are in the area at this time it's the ultimate *moulid* experience, however the road is officially closed to foreigners and you will need a lot of willpower and some luck to get through.

Shalatein

The last outpost before Sudan, 100 km south of Berenice, Shalatein is not easily accessible for independent travellers as the political situation remains sensitive due to the disputed border area and thus the police are rather twitchy. Getting here on public transport is almost 'mission impossible' through the numerous police checkpoints. The vast majority of visitors come on a day trip from the big hotels in either Marsa Alam or El-Quseir. Shalatein is very spread out, with a split between modern governmental/military buildings and the shanty town-like market area to the south. Homes and businesses are generally made of plywood, painted pale blue and green, peopled by white-clad men and invisible women. The few concrete constructions include a basic hotel and a domineering restaurant serving tour groups that pass through. The reason for visiting is the exceptional daily camel market that brings Sudanese herders to mingle with the Bashari, Ababda and Rashaida tribespeople who make up the main population of the town. The market is busiest on a Thursday when local traders are frantically wheeling and dealing before the weekend; consequently, Fridays are the least active time to visit (although the market does still operate), while most of the tourist groups come on Tuesday or Wednesday. While the Rashaida migrated from Saudi Arabia around 200 years ago, the Bashari belong to the nomadic Beja tribe who have been wandering the Red Sea hills for 6000 years, not answering to any central government until the early 1990s. Both tribes wear their traditional clothes like a uniform, Rashaida men in mauve *galabiyas* and the women in dark red dresses laden with jewellery, whilst Bashari men twist a fine length of cotton 4-7 m long around their heads to form a massive turban called an *ema*. Camels are traded between the locals and the squatting Sudanese who wear long knives and carry a camel whip and wooden bowl for watering their beasts; thousands of euro can be passed over the sand during these transactions. The current going price for a camel is E£6000-7000. Aside from the animal market, wooden stalls sell a huge variety of produce and products, intermingled among these are a few selling 'souvenirs' such as the silver, pottery, shields and swords that are still used in the daily routines of the tribespeople. An organized trip here is pricey, at around €80, but as it is presently the only easy way to visit this remarkable town it's money well spent.

◉ South of Hurghada listings

For sleeping and eating price codes and other relevant information, see pages 11-15.

◎ Where to stay

Safaga *p106*

€€€€ La Residence des Cascades, 48 km, Safaga Rd, T065-354 2333, www.residencedescascades.com. On the Soma Bay peninsula, renowned for the golf course (in which it stands) as much as for its Thalassotherapy centre, this hotel is wonderfully plush and has endless leisure facilities, as well as spectacular views and surroundings. Go online for the best prices.

€€€€-€€€ Menaville Resort, about 5 km north of Safaga port, T065-326 0064-7, www.menaville.com. A good 4-star choice. Chalets and villas in gardens, by pool or adjacent to the very good beach, all rooms a/c, telephone, minibar and terrace or balcony. Shops, bank, laundry, clinic. 24-hr café, cycle hire, billiards, table tennis. Has its own dive centre, www.menadive.com, with private jetty. Unlimited shore diving from hotel reef and boat dives available with all equipment for hire.

El-Quseir *p106*

There are a couple of excellent budget and mid-range options in El-Quseir that make for a memorable visit. Hotels in town don't have pools, but you can use the perfect beach at Rocky Valley Beach Camp, 14 km north, for E£20 per day, which includes a soft drink.

€€€ Flamenco Beach & Resort, 7 km north of town, T065-335 0200-9, www.flamencohotels.com. High-class resort on a beautiful stretch of beach, bustling but relaxed atmosphere, good food, and a couple of lovely pools. Generic architecture and room design, but worth checking online as you can score some great deals, especially in summer. Mainly Italian and German guests, snorkelling off the end of the pier.

€€€ Movenpick Resort, El-Quadim Bay, 5 km north of El-Quseir, T065-333 2100, www.moevenpick-hotels.com. Unbeatable value (book online) and one of the coastline's most stunning hotels with a coral reef running the entire length of the private beach. You can almost snorkel from your room. Moorish style, environmentally conscious, lovely gardens and beach, large pool, 3 restaurants of which **Orangerie** is recommended. Masses of activities on offer and Subex Dive Centre, see page 114.

€€-€ Al Quseir Hotel, Sharia Port Said, T065-333 2301. At the northern end of the harbour, this hotel of just 6 rooms in an old merchant's house is atmospheric and unusual, expect exposed brick walls and wonky stairs. Large rooms have little furniture (bed, wardrobe, sink, fan and a/c) but the wooden floors and ceilings and old doors with Islamic details make them special. On each floor there are 3 rooms that share 2 spacious bathrooms and, although relatively expensive for a real budget traveller, it's a place you won't forget. Breakfast is included and they are prepared to negotiate on price.

€€-€ Rocky Valley Beach Camp, Abu Sawatir, T065-333 5247, T010-653 2964, www.rocky valleydiverscamp.com. Probably the best eco-camp on the entire stretch of eastern coast, 10 pristine and tasteful huts with comfy beds are dotted up the hillside, with stunning views to the sea below. Some have private bathrooms, others share hot showers. There's good snorkelling and diving straight off the beach, where there's a café, simple huts (€5 per night, bring a sleeping bag), shade and loungers. It's candlelit at night (the generator goes on for a few hours every day) and they throw a great party by firelight if you're up for it. Has own dive centre, and perfect host Hassan El Assy also runs trips to the Eastern desert (see below). The only irritation is that the road runs

between the camp and the beach, though that is usually the case with any camp along this coast. A taxi costs E£20 from the bus station.
€€-€ Roots Camp, Abu Sawatir, T010-212 3414. Next door to **Rocky Valley Beach Camp** and not as attractively sited nor as welcoming, but it is cheaper and enjoys the same stretch of sand. Clean new wooden chalets have a/c and private bath, plus older palm/stone huts with floor-standing fans share bathrooms, all are simply furnished with natural tones. Bedouin seating area, beer E£15, plans for a dive centre, currently the area is a bit of a building site.
€ Sea Princess Hotel, south of town next to the petrol station, T065-333 1880. The only budget option in El-Quseir, the majority of rooms resemble prison cells and share rather grubby bathrooms (singles E£30, doubles E£50). However, there are 3 newer pricier rooms on the 2nd floor with en suite and a/c, much more acceptable though with hard beds and pillows. You're better off paying a bit more in the **Al Quseir Hotel** if you want to be in town. Staff don't speak much English but are pleasant.

Marsa Shagra p107

Though several establishments have sprouted up in these parts in recent years, the oldest among them is still at the top, both for its comfort, facilities and experience, as well for its environmental sensitivity.
€€€€-€€€ Ecolodge Shagra Village, reservations in Cairo T02-2337 1833, in Shagra, T012-244 9073, T012-244 9075 www.redsea-divingsafari.com. Set back from the beach to the west of the coast road (so as not to spoil the view), the construction in local red sandstone is very sympathetic. A central domed area containing all the main facilities is surrounded by chalets, huts and tents with lots of space. All are spotlessly clean and very comfortable but only the chalets have private bath. There is no pool or bar, but the bay boasts a stunning beach

with a fantastic house reef, good for shore dives and snorkelling. However, it is not in the isolated seclusion you might expect, as there are a cluster of resorts all around. The owner, Hossam Helmi, is a pioneer in the area, and one of the foremost environmentalists on the coast. He's also a diving enthusiast and knows the surrounding seas better than most. Extensive diving day-long safaris are organized from the hotel. 2 offshore dives cost €35 per person all inclusive.

Marsa Alam p108

Hossam Helmi (see Marsa Shagra above) has 2 other high-end camps, each with their own bay and live-aboards.
€€€€-€€€ Marsa Nakari, 18 km south of Marsa Alam, offers chalets, huts and tents.
€€€€-€€€ Wadi Lahami, 142 km south of Marsa Alam has chalets and tents. Diving safaris are organized with a 3-day live-aboard programme at €85 per person per day all inclusive (food and dive gear). They also have kite- and windsurfing facilities at Wadi Lahami. Reservations to both camps are made through the Cairo office, T02-2337 1833.
€€€ Aquarius, T010-646 0408, www.aquariusredsea.com. By far the most aesthetically pleasing of the camps, 18 circular rush peaked huts all have acacias planted outside, white linen, draped sail-effect interiors, camel wool blankets and rugs (but no fan, windows, or en suite). There are also larger bungalows with rustic furniture, bathrooms, fans – though the quirkiness of the huts might be more appealing. Either way, the rooms on the higher ground are breezier and the best choice. Electricity switched off 2400-0600 and 0900-1600. Full board the only option. Their **Aquarius Dive Centre** is fully equipped.
€€€ Shams Alam, reservation office in Cairo, T02-2417 0046, www.shamshotels. com. A comfortable resort, 50 km south of Marsa Alam, though the food is not highly rated. Accommodation is in pale pink

bungalow-like complexes with domed roofs. There's a nice private sandy beach with a bar and windsurfing, and a rather small freshwater pool with a bar. The **Wadi Gamal Dive Centre** nearby specializes in diving safaris to more remote reefs in the south and is recommended. Price includes half board.

Also recently sprung up is a stretch of old-style camps in Tondoba Bay, 14 km south of Marsa Alam. The camps are a 5- to 10-min walk from a wide expanse of beach and are vaguely eco-orientated, however they are generally quite expensive (compared to equivalents in Dahab, say). Call ahead and try to negotiate a deal as it's definitely a peaceful, friendly place to hang out for a couple of days even if you're not into diving. When hiring a taxi from the bus station in Marsa Alam, ask for '*Kilo Arbatarsha*' if the driver seems unsure where Tondoba is, and it should cost no more than E£25.

€€€-€€ Bedouin Valley, T02-2632 6665, T012-218 1427, www.southredsea.net. Cobbled stone chalets have wooden floors, proper furniture and tiled bathrooms with towels, plus there are standing fans. In landscaped rockery gardens, there's a *sheesha* corner for starlit chilling and in- and outdoor restaurants, but no alcohol. **South Red Sea** dive centre on the beach.

€€ Deep South, T012-450 1296, best views as on the highest ground and there's a cute wicker pub on site. Rooms are quite basic with beds and wardrobes being the only furniture, no fans, and all decorated with murals – some more lurid than others – giving a hippy-ish vibe. Clean, tiled shared bathrooms adjoin the open-air restaurant. New larger chalets have private baths. The food is highly recommended.

€ Emy Camp, T012-771 6023. The cheapest option in Tondoba are these simple, but sizable, white concrete chalets. All have fans, tiled floors, big beds and shared bath (though 6 huts are being constructed with private bath). Samir and Sara are laid-back and lovely

hosts, he used to sing in a rock band and ensures that there are always tunes playing. Meals are generous and tasty with an Oriental slant. Diving can be arranged.

Camping

€€€-€€ Fustat Wadi El Gemal, 45 km south of Marsa Alam, T012-240 5132, www.wadielgemal.com. A remote location 7 km inside one of Egypt's most beautiful and culturally fascinating national parks, this place makes a great base for anyone who has seen enough of the beach and wants to get back to nature. Striking tents (*'Fustat'* means 'tented camp') some with en suites, have very comfortable beds, or huts of traditionally woven palms are dotted around the austere desert landscape. Activities include trekking and camel trips (they also have camel wagons) and it's a chance to learn about tribal culture and the desert environment. The main dining tent, stylishly lit by a chandelier with huge bolster cushions to recline on, serves up great food and the breakfast is truly memorable. There's also a small bazaar selling handicrafts.

Shalatein *p109*

Should you manage to negotiate the transport difficulties and police checkpoints, there is a bearable hotel in Shalatein located right next to the market:

€ El Haramin, T016-653 1178. Large rooms cost E£40 without bath, or E£50 with private bath, both have a/c and fans. Cleanliness is not a high point, but rooms have balconies and clean sheets are provided on request. The location is ideal, with the camel market and eating options a short walk away.

🍴 Restaurants

Safaga *p106*
As Safaga is significantly less touristed than nearby Hurghada, most restaurants are confined to the hotels, as are the bars and discos. There are some cheap cafeterias

selling standard grilled fare along the main drag, Sharia Al-Gomhuriyya.

El-Quseir *p106*

Eating out in El-Quseir can be a delicious experience, particularly if you like fish. For standard food like *fuul* and *taamiyya*, look around the main market street. Any of the coffee shops lining the beach are cheap fun places to hang out in the evenings with decent *sheesha* and traditional drinks, but you might want to agree the price first.

€€ Al Quseir Hotel, T065-333 2301, has a good chef who (with advance warning) can put on a real spread with your choice of meat/fish/veggies for around E£70. The price goes down the bigger the group.

€€ El Ferdous Restaurant, at the north end of the harbour just before **Al Quseir Hotel**, is a great little fish restaurant with very reasonable prices. Choose between a clean a/c interior or seating on the beach. Fish is about E£35 per kilo, prawns E£140 or local grilled squid E£90. This is where the locals go for a treat, highly recommended.

€€ Marianne Restaurant, on the Corniche, T065-333 4386. Open 0800-2400. A more varied menu including Italian dishes, kebabs, and of course fish and calamari. Meals come with rice and salads, vegetarians are catered for, drinks moderately priced, and they sell cans of Saqqara for E£15. The upstairs balcony laden with bougainvillea and pottery urns is the best place to dine, otherwise there is beach seating, but note that the toilets leave a lot to be desired.

€€ Rocky Valley Beach Camp, T065-333 5247, T010-6532964, www.rockyvalleydivers camp.com. Call in the morning and you can state your preference for dinner, fabulous fresh fish and shrimps cooked on the grill, plus great salad, and beer is usually available. If you're lucky the delightful staff will get singing and dancing round the campfire later on, or you can just recline on cushions and watch for shooting stars as you digest.

€ Koshary El Mina, Corniche. This restaurant at the north end of the Corniche is more popular for its kebabs than its *koshari*.

Marsa Alam *p108*

Choices in the small village are very limited. Outside of the hotels and camps, there's really only one local café that's clean enough to warrant a recommendation. It's at the entrance to town on the right side of the main road, across from the port. Order whatever's on the stove.

Shalatein *p109*

There are a few local eateries in the market area serving meals for E£10-20, and in the camel *souk* itself there is a popular little shack that does good Egyptian breakfasts for rock-bottom prices. Otherwise, the 3-storey orange **Ristorante Basma Genoub**, T010-777 2184, on the main road near the market, open 1000-2400, does meals of camel meat, salad, rice and veg for E£50 including a soft drink. The 2nd floor with a domed ceiling and kitsch decor is the nicest.

⊙ Festivals

Marsa Alam *p108*

Oct/Nov Characters of Egypt Festival, this 3-day festival in Wadi El-Gemal National Park celebrates the different desert tribes of Egypt with traditional dancing, sports, music and camel racing. It is held in the spectacular wadi, where hundreds of participants and spectators can camp for the duration, see www.wadielgemal.com for details.

▲ What to do

Safaga *p106*

Diving

The best dive sites around Safaga are **Panorama**, where a sloping hill leads to a dramatic drop-off and sharks and mantas often linger; and **Abu Qifan**, a remote and pristine site that leaves behind the traffic of Hurghada live-aboards. The prolific marine life is an underwater photographer's dream. There are frequent sightings of dolphin, ray, barracuda, reef and leopard shark. All dive centres in Safaga organize day trips and half-day to the nearby sites. A standard PADI Open Water course, all inclusive, costs €350-380.

Barakuda, at Lotus Bay, 5 km north of Safaga, T065-326 0049, www.barakuda-diving.com. Have several centres around the Red Sea and a live-aboard.

MenaDive, T065-326 0060, www.menadive.com. A well-established, eco-conscious operation running out of the **Menaville Hotel**.

El-Quseir *p106*

Desert trips

Rocky Valley Tours, Sharia Port Said, just south of the Corniche, T065-333 5247, www.rockyvalleydiverscamp.com. Sat-Thu 1000-1500 and 1800-2300. Organize a range of short jeep safaris into the Eastern Mountains, some with a geological bent, for around €35 per night including Bedouin BBQ. 1-day hiking, half-day camel safaris to the village of Oum Hamid or trips to the camel market at Shalatein (€80) are also available. Pretty flexible and comparatively cheap.

Diving

Shallow dives Off the shore at **Movenpick's Subex Dive Centre**, www.subex.org (very professional and eco-conscious, but extremely expensive) is **El-Qadima Bay** with a variety of topography and fauna; about 10 km further south is the more sheltered **El-Kaf**.

Deep dives The islands **Big Brother** and **Little Brother** are about 1 km apart, 67 km off the shore northeast of El-Quseir. They were off limits for a few years until authorities developed a protection plan. They reopened in the late 1990s as part of a newly decreed Protected Marine Area. 2 exposed parts of the same reef, the Brothers offer what some say is the best diving in the Red Sea. Divers

pilgrimage to make the plunge, and special permission is required as the area is strictly regulated. Access is by live-aboard. The walls are a vertical 900 m. On Big Brother, the larger island, there's a stone lighthouse constructed by the British in 1883 (and still working). To the northwest of Big Brother are 2 wrecks. The unnamed cargo vessel with its shattered bow can be reached at 5 m (and then deeper as it is at an incline). The other wreck is **Aida II** (see page 54). The strong currents around Little Brother are home to vast fan corals and caves, and sharks are of various sorts are often seen. Along with stunning corals, these 2 dives offer an impressive range of fish.

Rocky Valley Beach Camp, Abu Sawatir, 14 km north of El-Quseir, have a good little set-up and run PADI Open Water courses for €310, including manual and certification, and 2 dives per day for €35. There is a reef off the beach for shore diving and they also rent snorkelling masks and fins for E£15 per day.

Marsa Shagra *p107*

Desert trips

Though most venture this far south for the underwater splendours, the desolate majesty of the desert is the ideal place for reflection and respite above ground. Hotels can help you organize jeep and horseback safaris into the surrounding mountains to visit nearby oases and a number of ghost cities created when the mines were abandoned. More in-depth exploration of the wadis, tribal villages and desert habitat is becoming possible.

Red Sea Desert Adventures, T012-230 9142, www.redseadesertadventures.com. Can organize anything from a day trek to a 2-week expedition visiting some extraordinary sites, many of which have yet to be fully uncovered. The season lasts from Oct-Mar; longer safaris require a minimum of 5 people and need to be booked at least a month in advance. Standard day-packages might include land-sailing, quad-riding, star-gazing camels and dancing performances (see the website for details of these).

Marsa Alam *p108*

Desert trips
Fustat Wadi El Gemal, T012-240 5132, www.wadielgemal.com. Wadi Gemal is a protected area south of Marsa Alam, and this eco-conscious set-up runs half-day camel safaris (€35 with a delicious dinner) or night safaris (€85) as well as day/night hiking trips. Much better is to immerse yourself for a few days in the enclave of the National Park. This provides a rare opportunity to trek into the Valley of the Camels or Wadi Sakhit, with a local Beja guide, for a day or few. Not only does this mean the chance of seeing ibex, gazelles and migratory birds but the scenery is stunning and savannah-like, and historical sites can be explored on the way. They also do 4WD trips for a minimum of 4 people.

Diving
At the **Abu Dabab** dive site, dugongs are seen on most days in the sea-grass, hence it is very popular. Too popular in fact, as the propellers of boats and hundreds of divers daily are causing stress to the ponderous beasts, who do not necessarily like being followed as they are trying to feed. Turtles, guitar sharks and rays are also frequent visitors. **Elphinstone Reef**, also known as Sharks' House as it's rare not to see one of 7 species, including tigers and hammerheads, 12 km off shore, only for experienced divers due to the depth; **Daedalus Reef**, 60/96 km off shore; **Sha'ab Samadai**, the Dolphin House, 5 km southeast in Marsa Alam National Park, comes with a 100% guarantee of seeing spinner dolphins. Entrance fees apply to the crescent-shaped reef and numbers are restricted to 100 divers and 100 snorkellers per day. There is also a no-human zone as efforts are made to protect the pod (which is very unusual in that it stays at the reef rather than the open ocean, as

spinners typically do). Divers cannot enter the lagoon but can dive around the outside of the reef, where there are caves and pinnacles of soft and hard coral; **Dolphine Reef**, 15 km to the northwest of Ras Banas; **Zabargad Island**, 45 km southeast of Berenice. Dive sites near Berenice are only accessible on live-aboard dive boats.

All the big resorts around Marsa Alam have their own dive centres, and there are 3 smaller outfits and a decompression chamber at Tondoba Bay, 14 km south of Marsa Alam, where there is a house reef. The following are both reputable and offer Open Water courses:
Aquarius, T010-646 0408, www.aquariusredsea.com.
Blue Heaven Holidays, T017-805 8885, www.blueheavenholidays.com. Offer a unique opportunity in Egypt for divers to get involved in reef conservation and monitoring efforts alongside marine scientists. It's a chance to enhance your own environmental knowledge while collecting valuable data that will aid the protection of the southern reefs. Visit their website to see when the next surveys are being undertaken.
South Red Sea Enterprises, T02-2635 2406, www.southredsea.net.
Wadi Gimal Diving Centre, T012-244 4931, wadigamal@shamshotels.com, 45 km south of Marsa Alam. Offer a wide variety of dive trips to unspoilt areas of the southern Red Sea including live-aboards.

⊖ Transport

Safaga *p106*

Bus
Buses via **Hurghada** (E£10) to **Suez** (E£20-40) every 1-2 hrs of which 5 go on to **Cairo** (7-8 hrs, around E£50). Buses to **Qena** (E£12-15), **Luxor** (E£25) and **Aswan** (E£30-35) 4-5 times a day. Buses to **El-Quesir** (2 hrs, E£8) and **Marsa Alam** (3 hrs, E£15) leave at 0600, 1600, 1900, 2100, 0200.

Ferry

Safaga is now one of the main departure points for vessels to Saudia Arabia since operations have virtually ceased from Suez. Sea passenger boats leave here for **Duba** daily. During the *hajj* there are passenger boats to **Jeddah** (not advised). Check at the port.

Taxi

Service taxis follow all the bus routes – change at **Suez** for **Cairo**. Prices are comparable to bus costs, but the journeys tend to be a bit faster (and more terrifying).

El-Quseir *p106*

Air

There is an international airport 70 km south of town that also serves **Marsa Alam**. Package tourists also fly in via **Hurghada**, 80 km north.

Bus

The bus station is about 2 km inland; frequent microbuses run from town along the Corniche continuing on to the bus station. Check all times and destinations as schedules change often. There buses to **Cairo** (8 hrs, E£85) via **Safaga** and **Hurghada** (2 hrs, E£15) at 0500, 1200 and 2000; 2 pass through **Suez** at 0500 and 2330 (6 hrs, E£25). There is 1 daily bus to **Qift** that departs at 0500. From there, you can easily find a bus or train to **Luxor** (1 hr) and **Aswan** (4 hrs). As with other cities on the coast, independent travellers bound for the Nile Valley on public buses are generally OK (ie won't get kicked off) if there are only 4 or less on board. There are also supposedly 4 buses per day to **Marsa Alam** (E£10, 2 hrs) and beyond at 0500, 0800, 1400, and 2130.

Service taxi

Service taxis and microbuses leave from a compound next to the bus terminal. They run all day (on a leave-when-full basis), and are reluctant to take foreigners. However, be insistent as, despite what drivers believe, the police do not fine services that take foreign passengers. You may, however, have to pay double the local fare. To **Marsa Alam**, E£10, 2 hrs; to **Qena**, E£12, 2 hrs; to **Safaga** 1½ hrs, E£5.50; to **Hurghada**, E£10, 2hrs; to **Qift**, E£16, 3 hrs. Change at **Suez** for **Cairo**.

Marsa Alam *p108*

Air

There is an international airport 60 km north of Marsa Alam that also serves **El-Quseir**.

Bus

To get out of Marsa Alam, ask the locals about the latest schedules once you get to town, as things change with the winds. At present, from Marsa Alam to **Cairo**, there are buses that stop in **Safaga** and **Hurghada** at 1000, 1500 1800 and 2000 (E£65); otherwise it's easy to catch a ride to Hurghada and transfer. Crossing the road to **Edfu** from Marsa Alam is difficult for tourists, as many drivers are wary of the 3 check points on the way, but if you want to try and trust the unspoken 4 tourists or less rule, the public bus heads west around 2400 and takes 4 hrs and carries on to **Aswan**, E£16, 3 hrs.

Taxi

Service taxis (Peugeot-style) run up and down the coast regularly, on a leave-when-full basis. They are comparable in price to the buses, but faster and more frequent, though again drivers can be obstructive to tourists. There are infrequent services throughout the day to **El- Quseir** (E£10, 2 hrs), where more northbound and westbound services/buses depart from.

Shalatein *p109*

Bus Buses leave from the *souk*, near the Ristorante Basma, and go via the bus station in town, to **Cairo** at 0700, 1430 and 1700 (E£85) via **Hurghada** and towns in between. To **Qena** at 0900 and 1100.

Contents

Footnotes

Basic Egyptian Arabic for travellers

It is impossible to indicate precisely in the Latin script how Arabic should be pronounced so we have opted for a very simplified transliteration that will give the user a sporting chance of uttering something that can be understood by an Egyptian.

Greetings and farewells

Hello	*ahlan wasahlan/*
	assalamu aleikum
Goodbye	*ma'a el salama*
How are you?	*Izayak?* (m); *Izayik?* (f)
Fine	*kwayis* (m) *kwayissa* (f)
See you tomorrow	*Ashoofak bokra* (m)
	Ashoofik bokra (f)
Thank God	*il hamdullil'allah*

Basics

Excuse me	*law samaht*
Can you help me?	*Mumkin tisa'idny?* (m)
	Mumkin tisa'ideeny (f)
Do you speak English?	*Bitikalim ingleezy?* (m)
	Bitikalimy ingleezy? (f)
I don't speak Arabic	*Ma bakalimsh 'araby*
Do you have a problem?	*Fee mushkilla?*
Good	*kweyyis*
Bad	*mish kweyyis, wahish*
I/you	*ana/inta* (m); *inty* (f)
He/she	*howwa/heyya*
Yes	*aiwa/na'am*
No	*ia'a*
No problem	*mafeesh mushkilla*
Please	*min fadlak* (m)
	min fadlik (f)
Thank you	*shukran*
You're welcome	*'afwan*
God willing	*Insha'allah*
What?	*Eih?*
Where?	*Fein?*
Where's the bathroom	*Fein el hamam?*
Who?	*Meen?*
Why?	*Leih?*
How?	*Izay?*
How much?	*Bikam?*

Numbers

0	*sífr*
1	*wahad*
2	*etneen*
3	*talaata*
4	*arba*
5	*khamsa*
6	*sitta*
7	*saba'a*
8	*tamenia*
9	*tissa*
10	*ashra*
11	*hidashar*
12	*itnashar*
13	*talatashar*
14	*arbatashar*
15	*khamstashar*
16	*sittashar*
17	*sabatashar*
18	*tamantashar*
19	*tissatashar*
20	*'ayshreen*
30	*talaateen*
40	*arba'een*
50	*khamseen*
60	*sitteen*
70	*saba'een*
80	*tmaneen*
90	*tissa'een*
100	*mia*
200	*miteen*
300	*tolto mia*
1000	*alf*

Dates and time

Morning	*el sobh*
Afternoon	*ba'd el dohr*
Evening	*masa'*
Hour	*sa'a*

Day	*yom*
Night	*bil leil*
Month	*shahr*
Year	*sana*
Early	*badry*
Late	*mit'akhar*
Today	*inaharda*
Tomorrow	*bokra*
Yesterday	*imbarah*
Everyday	*kol yom*
What time is it?	*E'sa'a kam?*
When?	*Imta?*

Days of week

Monday	*el itnein*
Tuesday	*el talaat*
Wednesday	*el arba'*
Thursday	*el khamees*
Friday	*el goma'*
Saturday	*el sapt*
Sunday	*el had*

Travel and transport

Airport	*el matar*
Plane	*tayara*
Boat	*markib*
Ferry	*'abara*
Bus	*otobees*
Bus station	*mahatit otobees*
Bus stop	*maw'if otobees*
Car	*'arabiya*
Petrol	*benzeen*
Tyre	*'agala*
Train	*atr*
Train station	*mahatit atr*
Carriage	*karetta; calesh*
Camel	*gamal*
Donkey	*homar*
Horse	*hosan*
Ticket office	*maktab e'tazakir*
Tourist office	*makta e'siyaha*
I want to go…	*a'yiz arooh* (m)
	a'yiza arooh (f)
Does this go to…	*da beerooh*
City	*madeena*
Village	*kareeya*

Street	*shari'*
Map	*khareeta*
Passport	*gawaz safar*
Police	*bolice*

Directions

Where is the…	*fein el …*
How many kilometres is …	*kem kilometers el …*
Left	*shimal*
Right	*yimeen*
After	*ba'ad*
Before	*'abl*
Straight	*doghry; ala tool*
Near	*gamb*
Far	*bi'eed*
Slow down	*bishweish*
Speed up	*bisora'*
There	*hinak*
Here is fine	*hina kwayis*

Money and shopping

25 piasters/a quarter pound	*robe' gineih*
Bank	*benk*
Bookstore	*maktaba*
Carpet	*sigada*
Cheap	*rikhees*
Do you accept visa?	*Mumkin visa?*
Do you have…	*'andak …* (m); *andik …* (f)
Exchange	*sirafa*
Expensive	*ghaly*
Gold	*dahab*
Half a pound	*nos gineih*
How many?	*kem?*
How much?	*bikem?*
Jewellery	*seegha*
Market	*souk*
Newspaper in English	*gareeda ingleeziya*
One pound	*gineih*
Silver	*fada*
That's too much	*kiteer awy*
Where can I buy…	*fin ashtiry…*

Food and drink

Beer	*beera*
Bread	*'aysh*
Chicken	*firakh*

Coffee	*'ahwa*
Coffee shop	*'Ahwa*
Dessert	*helw*
Drink	*ishrab*
Eggs	*beid*
Fava beans	*fu'ul*
Felafel	*ta'ameyya*
Fish	*samak*
Food	*akul*
Fruit	*fak ha*
I would like...	*a'yiz* (m); *a'yza* (f)
Juice	*'aseer*
Meat	*lahma*
Milk	*laban*
Pepper	*filfil*
Restaurant	*mata'am*
Rice	*roz*
Salad	*salata*
Salt	*malh*
Soup	*shorba*
Sugar	*sucar*
The check please	*el hisab law samaht* (m)
	samahty (f)
Tea	*shay*
Tip	*baksheesh*
Vegetables	*khodar*
Vegetarian	*nabaty*
Water	*maya*
Water pipe	*shisha/sheesha*
Wine	*nibeet*

Accommodation

Air conditioning	*takeef*
Can I see a room?	*Mumkin ashoof owda?*
Fan	*marwaha*
Hotel	*fondoq*
How much is a room?	*Bikam el owda?*
Is breakfast included?	*Fi iftar?*
Is there a bathroom?	*Fi hamam?*
Room	*oda*
Shower	*doush*

Health

Aspirin	*aspireen*
Diarrhea	*is hal*
Doctor	*dok-tor*
Fever	*sokhoniya*
Hospital	*mostashfa*
I feel sick	*ana 'ayan* (m) *ana 'ayanna* (f)
I have a headache	*'andy sod'a*
I have a stomache ache	*'andy maghas*
I'm allergic to	*'andy hasasiya*
Medicine	*dawa*
Pharmacy	*saydaliya*

Useful words

Church	*kineesa*
Clean	*nadeef*
Cold	*bard*
Desert	*sahara*
Dirty	*wisikh*
Hot	*har*
Less	*a'al*
More	*aktar*
Mosque	*gami'*
Mountain	*gabal*
Museum	*el mathaf*
River	*nahr*
Sandstorm	*khamaseen*
Sea	*bahr*
Summer	*seif*
Valley	*wadi*
Winter	*shita*

Dodging touts

You'll get hassled less and respected more if you learn a bit of Arabic.

no thank you!	*La'a shocrun*
I told you no!	*U'ltilak la'a*
I don't want;	*Mish ay-yez* (m)
I'm not interested	*mish ay-zza* (f)
enough	*Bess*
finished, that's it	*Khalas*
'when the apricots bloom' (ie 'in your dreams')!	*F'il mish mish*

Glossary

A

Abbasids Muslim Dynasty ruled from Baghdad 750-1258

Agora Market/meeting place

Aïd/Eïd Festival

Aïn Spring

Almohads Islamic Empire in North Africa 1130-1269

Amir Mamluk military officer

Amulet Object with magical power of protection

Ankh Symbol of life

Apis bull A sacred bull worshipped as the living image of Ptah

Arabesque Geometric pattern with flowers and foliage used in Islamic designs

B

Bab City gate

Bahri North/northern

Baladiyah Municipality

Baksheesh Money as alms, tip or bribe

Baraka Blessing

Barbary Name of North Africa 16th-19th centuries

Basha See Pasha

Basilica Imposing Roman building, with aisles, later used for worship

Bazaar Market

Bedouin Nomadic desert Arab

Beni Sons of (tribe)

Berber Indigenous tribe of North Africa

Bey Governor (Ottoman)

Borj Fort

Burnous Man's cloak with hood – tradional wear

C

Caid Official

Calèche Horse-drawn carriage

Canopic jars Four jars used to store the internal organs of the mummified deceased

Capital Top section of a column

Caravanserai Lodgings for travellers and animals around a courtyard

Cartouche Oval ring containing a king's name in hieroglyphics

Chechia Man's small red felt hat

Chotts Low-lying salt lakes

Colossus Gigantic statue

D

Dar House

Darj w ktaf Carved geometric motif of intersecting arcs with super-imposed rectangles

Deglet Nur High quality translucent date

Delu Water-lifting device at head of well

Dey Commander (of janissaries)

Dikka Raised platform in mosque for Koramic readings

Djemma Main or Friday mosque

Djin Spirit

Dólmenes Prehistoric cave

Dour Village settlement

E

Eïd See Aïd

Eïn See Aïn

Erg Sand dune desert

F

Faqirs Muslim who has taken a vow of poverty

Fatimids Muslim dynasty AD 909-1171 claiming descent from Mohammed's daughter Fatimah

Fatwa Islamic district

Fellaheen Peasants

Felucca Sailing boat on Nile

Fondouk/Funduq Lodgings for goods and animals around a courtyard

Forum Central open space in Roman town

Fuul Fava beans

G

Gallabiyya Outer garment with sleeves and a hood – often striped

Garrigue Poor quality Mediterranean scrubland

Gymnasium Roman school for mind and body

H

Haikal Altar area

Hallal Meat from animals killed in accordance with Islamic law

Hamada Stone desert

Hammam Bath house

Harem Women's quarters

Harira Soup

Hypogeum The part of the building below ground, underground chamber

I

Iconostasis Wooden screen supporting icons

Imam Muslim religious leader

J

Jabal See Jebel

Jami' Mosque

Janissaries Elite Ottoman soldiery

Jarapas Rough cloth made with rags

Jebel Mountain

Jihad Holy war by Muslims against non-believers

K

Ka Spirit

Khedivate The realm of Mohammed Ali and his successors

Kilim Woven carpet

Kif Hashish

Kissaria Covered market

Koubba Dome on tomb of holy man

Kufic Earliest style of Arabic script

Kuttab Korami school for young boys or orphans

L

Lintel Piece of stone over a doorway

Liwan Vaulted arcade

Loculus Small compartment or cell, recess

M

Mahboub Coins worn as jewellery

Malekite Section of Sunni Islam

Malqaf Wind vent

Maquis Mediterranean scrubland – often aromatic

Marabout Muslim holy man/his tomb

Maristan Hospital

Mashrabiyya Wooden screen

Mastaba Tomb

Mausoleum Large tomb building

Medresa School usually attached to a mosque

Médina Old walled town, residential quarter

Mellah Jewish quarter of old town

Menzel House

Mihrab Recess in wall of mosque indicating direction of Mecca

Minaret Tower of mosque from which the muezzin calls the faithful to prayer

Minbar Pulpit in a mosque

Mosque Muslim place of worship

Moulid Religious festival – Prophet's birthday

Moussem Religious gathering

Muezzin Priest who calls the faithful to prayer

Mullah Muslim religious teacher

Murabtin Dependent tribe

N

Necropolis Cemetery

Noas Shrine or chapel

Nome District or province

O

Oasis Watered desert gardens

Obelisk Tapering monolithic shaft of stone with pyramidal apex

Ostraca Inscribed rock flakes and potsherds

Ottoman Muslim Empire based in Turkey 13th-20th centuries

Ouled Tribe

Outrepassé Horse-shoe shaped arch

P

Papyrus (papyri) Papers used by Ancient Egyptians

Pasha Governor

Phoenicians Important trading nation based in eastern Mediterranean from 1100 BC

Pilaster Square column partly built into, partly projecting from, the wall

Pisé Sun-baked clay used for building

Piste Unsurfaced road

Pylon Gateway of Egyptian temple

Pyramidion A small pyramid shaped cap stone for the apex of a pyramid

Q

Qarafah Graveyard

Qibla Mosque wall in direction of Mecca

R

Rabbi Head of Jewish community

Ramadan Muslim month of fasting

Reg Rock desert

Ribat Fortified monastery

Riwaq Arcaded aisle

S

Sabil Public water fountain

Sabkha Dry salt lake

Saggia Water canal

Sahel Coast/coastal plain

Sahn Courtyard

Salat Worship

Saqiya Water wheel

Sarcophagus Decorated stone coffin

Sebkha See Sabkha

Semi-columnar Flat on one side and rounded on the other

Serais Lodging for men and animals

Serir Sand desert

Shadoof Water lifting device

Shahada Profession of faith

Shawabti Statuette buried with deceased, designed to work in the hereafter for its owner

Shergui Hot, dry desert wind

Sidi Saint

Souk Traditional market

Stalactite An ornamental arrangement

of multi-tiered niches, like a honeycomb, found in domes and portrals

Stele Inscribed pillar used as gravestone

Suani Small, walled irrigated traditional garden

Sufi Muslim mystic

Sunni Orthodox Muslims

T

Tagine/tajine Meat stew

Taifa Sub-tribe

Tariqa Brotherhood/Order

Thòlos Round building, dome, cupola

Triclinium A room with benches on three sides

Troglodyte Underground/cave dweller

U

Uraeus Rearing cobra symbol, sign of kingship

V

Vandals Ruling empire in North Africa 429-534 AD

Vizier Governor

W

Wadi Water course, usually dry

Waqf Endowed land

Wikala Merchants' hostel

Wilaya/wilayat Governorate/district

Z

Zaouia/zawia/zawiya Shrine/Sennusi centre

Zellij Geometrical mosaic pattern made from pieces of glazed tiles

Zeriba House of straw/grass

Index

Titles available in the Footprint *Focus* range

Latin America	UK RRP	US RRP
Bahia & Salvador	£7.99	$11.95
Buenos Aires & Pampas	£7.99	$11.95
Costa Rica	£8.99	$12.95
Cuzco, La Paz & Lake Titicaca	£8.99	$12.95
El Salvador	£5.99	$8.95
Guadalajara & Pacific Coast	£6.99	$9.95
Guatemala	£8.99	$12.95
Guyana, Guyane & Suriname	£5.99	$8.95
Havana	£6.99	$9.95
Honduras	£7.99	$11.95
Nicaragua	£7.99	$11.95
Paraguay	£5.99	$8.95
Quito & Galápagos Islands	£7.99	$11.95
Recife & Northeast Brazil	£7.99	$11.95
Rio de Janeiro	£8.99	$12.95
São Paulo	£5.99	$8.95
Uruguay	£6.99	$9.95
Venezuela	£8.99	$12.95
Yucatán Peninsula	£6.99	$9.95

Asia	UK RRP	US RRP
Angkor Wat	£5.99	$8.95
Bali & Lombok	£8.99	$12.95
Chennai & Tamil Nadu	£8.99	$12.95
Chiang Mai & Northern Thailand	£7.99	$11.95
Goa	£6.99	$9.95
Hanoi & Northern Vietnam	£8.99	$12.95
Ho Chi Minh City & Mekong Delta	£7.99	$11.95
Java	£7.99	$11.95
Kerala	£7.99	$11.95
Kolkata & West Bengal	£5.99	$8.95
Mumbai & Gujarat	£8.99	$12.95

Africa	UK RRP	US RRP
Beirut	£6.99	$9.95
Damascus	£5.99	$8.95
Durban & KwaZulu Natal	£8.99	$12.95
Fès & Northern Morocco	£8.99	$12.95
Jerusalem	£8.99	$12.95
Johannesburg & Kruger National Park	£7.99	$11.95
Kenya's beaches	£8.99	$12.95
Kilimanjaro & Northern Tanzania	£8.99	$12.95
Zanzibar & Pemba	£7.99	$11.95

Europe	UK RRP	US RRP
Bilbao & Basque Region	£6.99	$9.95
Granada & Sierra Nevada	£6.99	$9.95
Málaga	£5.99	$8.95
Orkney & Shetland Islands	£5.99	$8.95
Skye & Outer Hebrides	£6.99	$9.95

North America	UK RRP	US RRP
Vancouver & Rockies	£8.99	$12.95

Australasia	UK RRP	US RRP
Brisbane & Queensland	£8.99	$12.95
Perth	£7.99	$11.95

For the latest books, e-books and smart phone app releases, and a wealth of travel information, visit us at:
www.footprinttravelguides.com.

footprinttravelguides.com

Join us on facebook for the latest travel news, product releases, offers and amazing competitions: www.facebook.com/footprintbooks.com.